Paperback ISBN: 979-8-86-592615-3
Hardcover ISBN: 979-8-86-593004-4

BECOMING YOUR GREATER PURPOSE

Mindset Training to Get What You Want & Reach Your Full Potential.

Jeff Bennington

Praise For Becoming Your Greater Purpose:

"Jeff is a gifted storyteller. He writes with brutal honesty, sharing his hard-won lessons of growing up in the Midwest. His writing style is authentic and sincere. I could not put it down. He uses self-effacing humor that pulls you into his orbit, in a homespun style. It's like sitting on the front porch swing listening to your favorite uncle spin a year. Buy this book and give copies to the people you care about. They will thank you."

Mark Matteson, international speaker, best-selling author and podcaster.

Dedicated to anyone seeking their purpose.

Table Of Contents

Part 1

THE PROCESS OF BECOMING

"Becoming is better than being."

Carol S. Dweck

Chapter 1

WHAT ARE YOU BECOMING?

"It is not what we get, but who we become and what we contribute that gives meaning to our lives."

Tony Robbins

We are all born perfectly vulnerable, in an imperfect world. Somewhere along the way, the person you were designed to become got lost. The unique person created for a specific purpose – to bring value to the world at this specific time and place – was transformed into something else: a different person with fears, insecurities or a lack of purpose. The influence of others, their attitudes, words and actions, slowly but surely transformed your mindset into something more like them – more like those who had influence over you. Or, if you ventured too far on the side of unhealthy behavior, you may have created your own misery. Whether it was by a family member, bully or broken relationship, there are pieces of us that were stolen, damaged or changed – pieces that we may never know again. Through much of your existence, you've had this deep-seated feeling that who and what you've become isn't fully you. Oh, you get a glimpse of your greatness, on that rare occasion, but you know there's something missing; there's something inside of you that doesn't fit, and you just can't put your finger on it.

With over eight billion people on Earth, your story is one of a kind. Your friends and family, coworkers, influencers, culture and experiences have contributed to your uniqueness, and your belief system. They have inspired you, or maybe instilled a deep sense of anger or fear. You cherish the good things they have brought into your life, for sure; the positive and enriching gifts they have given. The harmful and painful memories have impacted you, too, perhaps even more so. Sometimes, the ideas that were so deeply ingrained in you resulted in a pessimistic view of the world, or caused you to distrust people, or see yourself as incompetent, in spite of your successes. Or maybe their influence made you stronger, confident and resilient.

In most cases, these are the people who contributed to your childhood development – family, friends, coaches, teachers, media personalities – and it is their combined view of the world that played a significant role in your development. With time and repetition, their attitudes, belief systems and mindsets rubbed off on you, to some degree. When this occurred, they became part of you. Unbeknownst to your younger self, your influencers influenced your ideas. Suddenly, the blank slate you began with was littered with messages that you have come to believe as true. Their perception of the world was transferred to you. Their ideas of success, money, relationships, marriage, character, communication, work and your personal potential permeated your belief system. When this happened, you started to see the world not as it is, but as you were told it is, and you began to take a path in life not measured by the person you were designed to become but, rather, by what could be the misguided beliefs of others.

Your destiny, therefore, can be subconsciously interwoven with the beliefs passed on to you. You may have been told that you have unlimited potential by a teacher, for example, but if a more powerful influencer communicated that society gives certain benefits to some people but not to you, that belief will take root and become your truth. This is how the ideas you heard growing up can tend to lead your life, even if they are not necessarily true. In other words, your beliefs were influenced by other people's beliefs. Somewhere in that influential stew, your beliefs and perceptions about life were baked in.

Another example of this transference of beliefs is when a child is told that she "can't afford" certain experiences:

"Mom, can I go on the field trip?"

"No, we can't afford it."

"Dad, can I go to soccer camp?"

"No, we can't afford it."

Meanwhile, other children, whose families are in the same financial condition, are given a different message, like: "We don't have the money right now, but what can you do to earn it?" In this case, the child learns a different way of viewing life. She calls Grandma, or puts up a lemonade stand, or babysits for extra money. In these contrasting scenarios, one child learns that money is scarce, and that belief carries over, long after she is an adult. The other child grows up to believe that, if she is resourceful and works hard, anything is possible. Similar conditions, different results.

This plays out in other parts of your life. Labels like "smart", "athletic", "dumb" or "clumsy" can influence how you see yourself, too. You become distrustful in relationships when you're trained that those closest to you can destroy your sense of safety. Beat in the idea that women can't be trusted, and a young boy, who loves his mother, becomes a misogynist. Tell your daughter, over and over, that her opportunities are limited, and that's what she'll experience. However, if she loves business, and is encouraged to follow in the footsteps of self-made female millionaires and female CEOs, she can learn to replicate their success.

Unfortunately, the ideas that were transferred to you can dictate where you're going in life. One of the greatest tragedies is when a vision for your life emerges, but the beliefs that were transferred to you nudge you down a path you didn't want to take. False beliefs about oneself frustrate many people, because they believe what they were taught is the absolute truth. This is not so.

Whether you accept it or not, your beliefs about yourself, others and the world around you impact every area of your life. They have governed your past, present and, potentially, your future. As long as you continue to believe the same messages and respond to life with the exact same thoughts and patterns, you will remain on the same course. Guided by your mindset, you are the captain of your life. You may think others control your choices and results, but they do not. You see, if you want to become your greater purpose and get what you want, you must align your goals and actions with your thoughts and beliefs. Often, what you actually want is in your left hand, but what you think about is in your right. You know what's in your left hand, but you have chosen to focus on the right hand: the drama, the social media, daily struggles, Netflix, scrolling on your phone; everything except what's in your left hand.

If what you want is in opposition to the things you focus on, your dreams will seem mysteriously out of reach. You'll start to believe that what you want just isn't in the cards for you. And you'll seek out the voices that reaffirm those beliefs, because it's too painful to believe that you are responsible for your inability to reach your goals.

Things like money, security, fulfillment and love are only as accessible as you think they are. Therefore, unless you change your mindset, you will forever hear that still, soft voice whispering that there's something better for you, that that child wired to make a unique contribution to the world is still here, hoping that someday your dreams will come true. Yet, when you clear away the clutter, and strip away the beliefs that have limited your potential, you may find a vision that gives you purpose and meaning, independent of what others think.

Your story is powerful, and there is always room for another chapter. Your story has brought you where you are today, and there are many lessons that have made you stronger, resilient and capable. But there are harmful beliefs that may have limited you, too. Your thoughts guide your mindset and your capacity or inability to move forward, to reach your goals or to take necessary risks. You may have spent years, or maybe decades, massaging those familiar beliefs, keeping you where you feel most comfortable. Or perhaps you're doing well, but missing one piece of the puzzle: that final piece that will send you soaring. It's my hope that this book helps you to find it. If you're willing to seek answers and consider new possibilities, everything could change for you, if that's what you want.

Throughout this book, I'll tell the stories that made me who I am. Stories like that of the bully from my freshman year in high school, who tormented me one too many times. After stepping on my white jeans with his dirty shoes, as he passed me on the bus, I finally summoned the courage to let him have it. Okay, I didn't really let him have it – I weighed 120 pounds soaking wet, and he was a 160-pound wrestler – but I fought back! The next day, I walked into math class and was greeted by my nemesis with a joke about my black eye. I kindly let my classmates know of the shiner that he was hiding, and that was the last time he bothered me. Stories like these will remind you of who you are, and help you put into perspective the person you are becoming.

As we embark upon this journey together, I hope you envision your stories along the way, so that you can learn how to transform limiting beliefs into a limitless reality, get what you actually want from life and become your greater purpose. Notice that I didn't say "discover" your purpose. I didn't say "find" your purpose. Your greater purpose isn't a light switch that you can turn on and off; it's a journey. It's an ultra-marathon. It's the entire process of living.

Your life is like a novel, in which you have the power to alter the traits of the protagonist, as she becomes the person capable of overcoming insurmountable odds. Until the ink dries on the novel of your life, there is always time for a turn of events, plot twists and exciting surprises. These are simply edits and revisions. Of course, there are some chapters that can never be erased, but you can always amend your story. When you understand this, you can embrace your past for what it was, forgive those who have hurt you, and work to become the person you were designed to become.

How do you become your greater purpose? Well, put on your backpack, bring some tissues and a hiking stick, because the terrain is treacherous indeed. You and I are going to traverse through my story (and yours) and discover what made you unique, examine how your belief systems were reinforced, and then how you can transform those beliefs, as rigid and cemented as they may seem, into a belief system with endless possibilities. By walking through our stories together, you will discover that we have much in common.

You may not believe that you are worthy of a greater purpose. You may have feelings of inadequacy or a lack of self-worth. Perhaps your family or other influencers have left you feeling incapable of accomplishing big dreams. Let me assure you that you are not alone. Your desire to be a part of something meaningful is natural. And, if you don't feel equipped or capable, that's okay. You are about to learn how real people, like me, who have felt ashamed and aimless for much of their life, become their greater purpose. We are all becoming someone. The question is, who are you becoming?

Becoming a greater purpose is for everyone; students, employees, rich, middle-class, poor, married, single, young or old – it doesn't matter who you are or where you come from, ultimately everyone is seeking a greater purpose. Elon Musk made hundreds of millions of dollars at a young age, and can have anything he wants, but he has chosen to live in a small house in Texas, where he's focused on his greater purpose, accelerating the world's transition to sustainable energy. Kylie Jenner supports Smile Train, helping children with clefts. Jeff Bezos has a foundation that supports childhood learning and education. But you don't have to be one of the richest people in the world to search for a deeper meaning. Elon, Kylie and Jeff demonstrate how money in itself is not enough to give us the fulfillment we seek. After acquiring all the cash they'll ever need, Kylie, Jeff and Elon still long for something meaningful enough to live for. We all do.

Living a greater purpose is your response to the problems you see in your little corner of the world. Tim Ballard is passionate about saving abused and enslaved children. Chad Pregracke has made it his life's mission to clean up the Mississippi River. Kaitlin Gregg Goodman is passionate about running joyfully and public health. Texas high-school-football coach, W.T. Johnston, inspired his players and their small town to believe in themselves and a higher power. Of course, many parents quietly raise their children to become their very best, not for notoriety, but out of love and the joy of seeing their children blossom. Teachers, first responders and public servants of all kinds give at the expense of wealth, because it must be done and they follow their heart. The men and women in skilled trades build and repair our homes and infrastructure because it must be done. Every generation faces new challenges. Every generation grows up in an ever-changing world. And yet, in spite of our many viewpoints, we're all still seeking a greater purpose and a life wrapped in meaning.

I spent decades searching for meaning. As a very spiritual person, I still felt lost and insecure, with no idea who I was or where I was going. I made many decisions as an adult, based on false beliefs about myself and the world around me, fumbling through life, chasing the wind. But I'm not alone. There are probably millions of people who feel the way I did, and that's why I'm so passionate about sharing what I've learned.

Over time, I've discovered that we all long for happiness, peace of mind, love, healthy relationships, financial security, experiences, rewarding challenges, a spiritual connection and the belief that we've made a difference in the world. And that belief, the hope that our existence is meaningful in some way, is a force that can drive our passions and frustrations. You see, we all have an internal mechanism that's seeking significance and meaning, but we don't always know what it's looking for. Sometimes we think it's money. Sometimes we think it's authority. Sometimes we think it's sex. Sometimes we think it's love. Sometimes we think it's fame, or glory, or accomplishments, or thrills. We get confused because of the messages we receive from family, the media and our influencers. But, ultimately, after the thrills and money and sex and power have waned, we are left longing. Longing for something greater. Longing for something we may not even understand.

You, too, may be longing for a greater purpose.

Why is it important for you to go on this journey? Why read this book? It's important because the drama of life will unfold quickly, and it will not wait for you to love, live and learn. You must do it while you can. Many people take their last breath on Earth thinking: *I should have loved more, I should have lived more, I should have discovered more.* The "should haves" in your life are the moments when you choose something other than your greater purpose. Steve Jobs once said: "Your time is limited, so don't waste it living someone else's life. Don't be trapped by dogma, which is living with the results of other people's thinking." The hours wasted on selfish pursuits or scrolling away on your smartphone will quickly sour as you lay on your deathbed, wishing you'd spent more time with loved ones and making a difference in the lives of others.

What's your purpose? What's your vision? What's the point of this life, anyway? These are the questions that we all ask ourselves at times, but the answers aren't simple. I believe that our individual (and collective) purpose is to discover why we're here, who we're meant to serve and how we're equipped to give that service. The challenge is to become fearlessly open to new experiences, so that you can uncover the answers. Becoming your greater purpose is not an amazing journey in your life; it's the amazing journey that *is* your life.

I have been inspired by and learned from many of the people I reference in this book. They have inspired and changed me in many ways, so I hope I can adequately pay it forward. Together, you and I will learn from them, and discover who you are at your core. I will ask some very difficult questions, and you will need to be thoughtful and honest.

This is not a prosperity mindset book. This is not a quick fix. This is not a get-rich-quick book. This book is exactly what it states: a book that can help you learn what it takes to get what you want, reach your full potential and become your greater purpose, with mindset training that will require effort on your part. I'm not a multimillionaire, or guru, or celebrity, I'm simply a writer living out his purpose, and for the duration of this book I'll be your guide and coach. I'm not perfect, and that will be apparent as you read the raw details of my transformation. I'm human and a work in progress. We all are.

I'll share my story along the way, because I think it's important for you to know that you're not the only one with struggles, anxieties and insecurities. Famous people like Jeff and Kylie and Elon don't seem to resonate with average people; we revere their accomplishments, but it's hard to relate to their bigger-than-life personas. Through my story, you'll see the exact process I went through, to go from aimless self-doubt to living my greater purpose. You'll learn the key principles that changed me, hear from my virtual mentors and learn the science behind mindset training. Like turning a key, the lessons in this book can open the door to a life you were meant to live.

The principles are universal and will not conflict with your spiritual beliefs. You will not have to sell your soul to get what you want and become your greater purpose. This book will enhance your spiritual beliefs, whatever they may be. As you work through the content, by answering the chapter review questions you'll evaluate your thoughts, habits and beliefs, and discover how they are impacting your possibilities. I'm excited to share my story, because I think it will play a small role in making your life more meaningful, and that is *my* greater purpose. Now, let's get to work!

Chapter review.

- What are the major takeaways for you in this chapter? How can you apply them to your life today?
- Why are you reading this book? What are you hoping to learn?
- Are you open to new ideas? When was the last time you tried something new or challenged your thinking?
- What does becoming your greater purpose mean to you?
- Do you believe someone, or an institution, is holding you back? Who and why?
- If you'd rather do something different with your life, what's stopping you?

Chapter 2

FEAR OF DEATH AND NEURAL PATHWAYS

"As you awaken, you will come to understand that the journey to love isn't about finding the one; the journey is about becoming the one."

Creig Crippen

Blood gushed out of my forehead while my mother frantically sopped it up with toilet paper, Kleenex, anything she could find to stop the deluge of vital fluid. My dad focused on the road, white-knuckling the steering wheel, and my three siblings sat in the back seat wondering what had just happened.

"Is he going to die?" my older sister asked.

"No," my mom replied.

As I lay in her lap, looking up at her, I could see the uncertainty in her eyes.

I could feel the warmth flowing down my face, after she removed a saturated rag from my forehead. I remember the taste of copper in my mouth. I felt weaker with every breath. When she found a fresh cloth, I'd whimper because it felt like it bit me every time she pressed it against my open wound. Before long, I blacked out, and that's all I remember.

I don't have any recollection of arriving at the hospital, surgery or my recovery. What I remember is that we were on vacation, or a weekend getaway, somewhere in Northern Michigan, and we pulled over for some reason; I think we were sightseeing. Maybe someone had to pee. I don't know why, but I recall my sister, two older brothers and I were running down a hill, racing, just having fun. There were trees everywhere. It was pretty. And I was moving fast. I must have aimed for the car because, when I jumped over the ditch, I slipped and my head slammed into the steel bumper. I'm sure I started crying, and it probably took a minute before anyone thought there was a serious problem; tears and loud noises were not uncommon in a household with four kids. Looking back, it was one of many ordeals, as I was an accident-prone boy.

Turns out that the emotions from that experience have been with me for more than forty years. There's a reason I remember that: the reason is because I was five years old and, as I lay there, staring at my mother's face, watching the pain and fear in her eyes, I felt her emotions and they made a deep impression on me. It was as if her fear of losing me was dripping from her soul, pouring directly into my heart. That moment is forever locked in the vault of my memories, embedded with physical pain, a visible scar and deep-seated emotions.

I lost my grandfather that same year. He was a lifelong smoker and died an early death, at the age of fifty-five. I was so heartbroken that they had to remove me from his funeral, because I was crying too loud. To this very day, I keep a picture of my grandpa and I fishing together in my office. Best I can recall, he was a calm voice in my life, at a time when there was so much chaos around me. There he sat, on the boat, holding his fishing rod, patiently watching his bobber, as I turned toward my dad – who was there, holding his camera – and then I smiled, blissfully loving life, happy to be a big boy on the boat. Bookstore Grandpa, as we called him, smoked a pipe, and I've always loved that earthy cherry-tobacco smell, because those were such wonderful memories.

Ironically, I've avoided any form of tobacco use for my entire adult life, due to the effects it had on my grandpa's health; that stuff killed him. However, while on a recent trip to Savannah, Georgia with my family, I walked into Ye Old Pipe Shop on the riverfront, because I was enticed by the glorious aroma; I couldn't help myself. I sniffed around and found a pipe, some tobacco and a few necessary tools that the shopkeeper recommended. Somehow I felt free to buy it. Several minutes later, after showing my father-in-law what I had purchased, I had an epiphany; I realized two important concepts that have been driving my life. Firstly, I concluded that I've had a fear of dying young, like my grandpa. As a result, the need for making an "impact" has been gnawing at me for decades. Secondly, the need to maintain a healthy lifestyle has undergirded many of my choices. And these subconscious forces, the best I know, were the result of losing my gramps, and possibly my perceived brush with death in my mother's arms. These are just two of many (perhaps thousands) of mindset drivers in my life.

So, how did that fear of death resolve itself? Well, I purchased that pipe on New Year's Eve, 2022. That evening, my family and I were gathered on a quaint front porch, in a historical Airbnb. As tradition goes, fireworks exploded in the distance, as Savannahians abroad celebrated the coming new year, by shooting bottle rockets and bullets into the air. I lit up that pipe, free from the fear of death, free from the fear of judgment and free of judging myself, too. I sat perfectly at peace on that front porch, in that beautiful neighborhood, and celebrated the memory of Bookstore Grandpa. It was a glorious New Year's Eve evening in Savannah.

That, dear friend, is how your brain develops: you experience or observe a situation, an emotion is triggered and a neural pathway is formed. And, that neural pathway – a unique neurological path (like an electrical circuit) formed in your brain – responds every time you find yourself in similar situations, over and over and over again. The more the experience occurs, the stronger the pathway. The stronger the emotion, coupled with repetition, the stronger the impact of that experience. Or, put another way, the stronger the emotional connection, the more control that circuit has over your response to daily circumstances. This is why, every time I smell the smoke from a pipe, I get nostalgic.

You have billions of neural pathways, many of which keep you alive, like breathing, your heartbeat, walking, listening and other physiological systems. The intensity in which you respond to stress is a neural pathway, too, but could also be construed as a habit. Like all neural connections, it's a circuit that cycles over and over, because it's familiar. The fear that builds inside when you're faced with a challenge arises in the same way. It's a neural connection that has been trained to protect you from the pain of failure. And you have other neural pathways that trigger when you're faced with difficult choices, anger and uncertainty.

Your thoughts and beliefs ingrained in your neural connections establish a mindset which, in turn, establishes your go-to response to life, how much risk you take, how far you develop your talents, your character, your relationships and how you navigate life in general. And your mindset determines what you believe is possible. This combination of mindset and neural pathways automates an output of thoughts which, in turn, drive your choices and actions and results. You could say that many of these pathways are subconscious drivers, but not all of them are hidden control systems. If you're like me, you can probably pinpoint a few beliefs that influence some of your choices, and you may even be capable of identifying when, where and by whom those beliefs were established.

This is true of all of us. Your vast experiences make you who you are today. The combination of unique experiences that brought joy, sadness, anger, pain, frustration, melancholy, hate and love caused your brain to form an endless number of neural connections, which trained you how to function according to your unique programming and upbringing. These neural connections form something like a supercomputer, that tells you how to respond to every <IF>/<THEN> situation you find yourself in, and this is generally established by the time you are seven or eight years old. Aristotle said: "Give me a boy until he is seven, and I will show you the man." It's an incredibly accurate developmental observation, understood long before neuroscience comprehended how the brain actually develops.

To put it simply, Harvard's Center for the Developing Child states: *"In the first few years of life, more than 1 million new neural connections are formed every second."*[1] Assuming a child sleeps for twelve hours, and experiences life for the other twelve hours, or 43,200 seconds, that equates to 43.2 billion new neural connections a day, or 15,768,000,000,000 new pathways in the first year of life. That's over fifteen trillion lines of code! Wow! To put that into perspective, Google has two billion lines of code. The Human Genome Project has 3,300 billion lines of code. When you add the emotions that reinforce a child's experiences, those connections have a powerful impact on your perception of life as a whole, which in turn establishes your overriding mindset. And this process continued throughout your adolescence. It's a cycle of experiential reinforcement that strengthens your "go to" response in every situation. Put another way, these reinforced neural connections become the way you respond to life. Your neural pathways, beliefs and thoughts dictate your everyday decisions, habits and actions, unless you consciously intervene.

It's no surprise that your self-concept and how you view the world are often determined at a young age, because you started with a clean sheet of paper. You knew nothing. Every experience was a question: can you trust the people around you? Is the world a kind place? Are you worthy of care? What is your attitude toward authority? Is it safe to play with other children? Is social interaction a risk, something to avoid? These seemingly childish concerns were reinforced, over and over, in whatever setting you were born into, and have serious implications for the way you view yourself, how you respond to conflict, how you see others and the world at large, lasting far into adulthood, perpetually dictating your choices and actions.

Your experiences and perceptions with the strongest emotions prevailed over lesser experiences. Whether those experiences painted an accurate picture of yourself, others and the world around you is immaterial; the beliefs that you accepted as true were reinforced and began to repeat – in your mind, anyway – over and over and over.

On the surface, this makes sense, but I don't think the majority of people think much about how their thoughts conflict with what they actually want.

The simplest example of this is how we think about money. People need and want money, usually not out of greed, but because they want something better for themselves and their family. However, your beliefs about money, most often established when you were young, can easily limit your ambitions and career success. This happens when you want more but, if you believe that wealthy people are crooks, greedy or have everything handed to them, you will avoid becoming something you despise, in spite of what you actually want.

This idea couldn't be more apparent than in the smash-hit song by Oliver Anthony, "Rich Men North of Richmond". The song praises the values of honest, hard-working Americans, and blasts the rich and powerful. There's no doubt that the lyrics point out several truths: that politicians are out of touch with middle America, have burned the dollar to the ground, and are tax- and power-hungry. I love the song, and I resonate with the ultimate message that big government is not kind to the middle class. But, what that song inadvertently does is reinforce a poverty mindset. Rather than showing people how to make a better life for themselves, regardless of corruption, it sets the listeners up to view rich people as evil. And yet, ironically, at the time of this writing, Mr. Anthony is making $40,000 a day from that song alone, not to mention performances and his other music. Is he evil? Of course not. But he is well on his way to becoming a millionaire. Oliver Anthony's song fortifies the culture of the poverty mindset, the idea that rich people are on one side of the aisle, while the rest of us are over here, powerless to change our fate. And that's simply not true; it's only true if that's what you believe. If you believe that you cannot make a better life for yourself, you won't. If you believe that you have to be greedy to become a millionaire, you may never experience financial freedom.

In my book, written for contractors, *HVAC Millionaire Mindset*, I define a poverty mindset as a desire for something better, obstructed by limiting beliefs. If you look for this mindset, you will see it play out all around you, every day. You'll notice how often people talk out of both sides of their mouth, complaining about the shape of their house, then spending hours watching television. Or people complaining about their income but doing nothing to improve their skills. Or adults complaining about their partner, yet never looking within to understand their role in the dysfunction.

The limiting beliefs in a poverty mindset tell you that you're powerless, because others are controlling your choices and financial results. If this is the case, then explain how immigrants coming into the United States with only the shirt on their back can succeed? The answer is that they have a mindset of hope. They have a growth mindset and take personal responsibility for getting what they want, in spite of the many obstacles ahead of them. The truth is that you are four times more likely to become a millionaire if you migrate to the United States. Think about the implications of that. If you have nothing to lose, you're more likely to get what you want... if you have the right mindset. If you start with less, you're more likely to get what you want – if you have the right mindset. If you take the pen away from others, you become the author of your life. Brene Brown put it this way: "If you own this story, you get to write the ending."

The mindset problem became apparent to me in the home services industry, when technicians proved over and over that they were capable of hitting sales targets immediately following sales training. Unfortunately, sales would wane after a month or so, because it was too exhausting for technicians to continue offering options and upgrades to homeowners, when their mindset was based on limiting beliefs about money and themselves. They call this "selling out of your own wallet". More accurately stated, it's the process of transferring one's beliefs about money onto the consumer. If a technician can't afford it, or if he wouldn't pay for the upgrades himself, the idea of paying more than it's worth to him impacted his willingness to offer the upgrade to the consumer. The irony in this scenario is that many technicians could double their income if they'd let go of their false beliefs about money. Yet, year after year, technicians complain about their income, hoping for a one- or two-dollar raise, when a much greater income is actually possible without overtime or extra effort, by simply letting the customer decide what options they want to buy.

It's quite possible that you could be living a similar situation, where you want more for your life, but you put that "want" into the hands of someone else: your employer, mate, family member, the government, etc. This is a form of self-sabotage. Your beliefs about life, money and value dictate who you believe is responsible for increasing your income, and your perception isn't necessarily true; it's just your perception. The truth is that you can increase your income, or position, or meaning in life, if you wish to make it so. When you leave your fate in the hands of someone else, you'll only get what they want. When you shift your focus to what you want, and take action in that direction, things will change.

After learning about the power of thinking habits, and making drastic changes in my life, I concluded there was no point in HVAC contractors spending thousands of dollars on sales training, until they address their technicians' mindsets first, because they will only perform well for a short period of time, unless they intentionally change their limiting beliefs. This is true for anyone in sales or performance-based work. If you employ a sales team, this is something you might seriously think about addressing. And, with the shortage of quality employees becoming an ever-increasing problem, mindset training will become more important to the future workforce. Tired of your employees' attitudes? They probably won't change by your firing or berating them; they need mindset training. And, maybe you do, as well.

The way you think about money is just one way your mindset impacts the direction your life can take. Another example relates to your career goals.

Practically speaking, if I asked if you'd ever consider applying for a management position in your company, what thoughts immediately come to mind?

I'll let you ponder that for a minute...

Did you think, *No, I haven't thought of that, but maybe I should,* or was your immediate response, *No, I could never do that,* or, *That's not my personality,* or, *I'm not qualified,* or, *No, I'm not a leader or a manager type,* or _____ *(fill in the blank objection)?* Maybe you thought, *No, but I wonder what it would take for that to happen?* Well, if that job pays more and you feel like you deserve more money from your employer, it would behoove you to learn some new skills to upgrade to that position, right?

I'd love to know what your initial response was. But, for the sake of this exercise, consider whether your response was open or closed to moving toward that ambitious goal. There's definitely truth in the idea that many people are not immediately qualified, or even want to become a leader. However, you could ask a number of similar questions, like:

- Would you start your own business?
- Should you go to college or get a trade?
- Would you consider sharing your story as a public speaker?
- Would you commit to starting a 30-day mindset challenge?

Whatever your response, it's quite likely that you'd give a similar answer, with similar reasons or excuses, that you've used to block, inhibit or otherwise manage your potential, based on your beliefs about yourself, others and how you view the world.

Take a minute and think about the decisions you've made based on your insecurities, fears and false beliefs. Was there a career path you wanted to take, but chose an easier route because you didn't think you were capable? Were you in love with someone and never told them, because you were afraid of rejection? Have you always dreamed of doing something exciting, but felt someone was holding you back? Perhaps that exercise reminds you of a time when you were working toward a dream and raised a few questions of your own, but the answers you gave yourself were less than encouraging? Do you look back at that time with regret? Can you see how your mindset impacted the decisions you've made?

We blame ourselves. We blame others. We wish things were different and feel disempowered to change. Is it any wonder that many adults are perpetually frustrated? Is it any wonder that people complain so much about their job, lot in life, income, car, house, spouse? Maybe you feel a lack of power over your circumstances, too?

Have you ever wondered why you keep doing or saying the same stupid things, over and over again? You know, losing your temper, or when you're overly critical, or when you're controlling or overly passive? Most of us have something that we know we should overcome. I've felt that way, too, and it was frustrating, because I felt powerless to change my circumstances.

For decades, I responded to stressful arguments with my wife with silence. If our argument became too heated, I didn't blow up; I shut up, sometimes for days. And that silence might just as well have been a punch in her face, because my response was equally painful to her. By disengaging from a meaningful conversation, my emotional withdrawal demonstrated that I didn't care about her feelings, thereby having the same emotional impact as if I had physically hurt her. I didn't want to do that. I felt like there was this dark web that overcame me, leaving me unable to break out. I have since come to realize that my response was nothing more than a triggered neural pathway; every time I'd go quiet, I was reinforcing that neural connection. I believe I learned to respond to stress like that because, when I was young, it became quite clear that if I'd "get smart", or "talk back", or express myself in any way contrary to what was expected of me (to be nice and be quiet), I'd receive a punishment, sometimes as harsh as being forced to drink a tablespoon full of raw tabasco sauce. If not that, I observed thousands of hours of dysfunctional communication between my parents, which likewise programmed my understanding of marital connection and relationships. Today, I have to consciously interrupt that pathway with a new response, force myself to talk and, shortly after, my physiological response to the stress relaxes and I'm better equipped for a conversation. Creating a new stress response – or overcoming any dysfunction, for that matter – takes time and repetition.

Why am I telling you this? And what does any of it have to do with becoming your greater purpose? The answer is simple: in the same way that there are tools for success, which many people aren't aware of (and we'll get into those), there are neural pathways and habits that may be preventing you from getting what you want, and you may not have any idea what is actually holding you back. For many people, these are the fears and subconscious garbage that keep you from changing careers, starting a business or taking that leap of faith you've always dreamed about. Unfortunately, your story can get in the way of accomplishing what you actually want out of life. Blaming others, your habits and what you think about could be some of your roadblocks. These muddy your path and make getting what you want more difficult than it otherwise is.

Therefore, if you're seeking something better for your life, you must evaluate your mindset first, because the world is what it is, and not necessarily as you perceive it. So, you must be honest about how you view life and the world around you before you attempt to become your greater purpose. Becoming your greater purpose requires you to understand who you are, and it requires that you understand how your mindset impacts the decisions you make. It requires you to understand that you are, in fact, the author of your life.

As Carl Jung said: *"Who looks outside, dreams; who looks inside awakes."* [2] By looking inward, Jung suggests that we embrace our "shadow": the darker, subconscious part of us that is doing the negative self-talk. He added: *"Everyone carries a shadow, and the less it is embodied in the individual's conscious life, the blacker and denser it is."*

I was introduced to my shadow after lying to my wife about a financial decision I made. There was no reason for it; a conversation beforehand would have sufficed, eliminating the problem. Why I lied baffled me. It was one of many times I've asked, out of frustration with myself: "Why do I do that?"

We all have a shadow, the part of us that we keep caged – our critical thoughts, judgments, lies we tell ourselves and our darkest desires – such that, if the world knew our thoughts and yearnings, they would surely despise us. You have a shadow, too, and a persona, and other parts of your personality that you allow the public to see, and other parts that you hide. Understanding and embracing all of these parts of you – your light and dark sides – is the beginning of understanding your true self, your strengths and weaknesses, and then how to move forward.

Understanding your mindset is the starting point, because it means that you have come to terms with your false beliefs. It means that you have succumbed to the knowledge that, outside of the hand of God, you are the master of your destiny. If you have a fixed mindset, like I did, you're convinced that the way things are is how they will always remain. Thoughts like, *I'm such an idiot... I'm so stupid... I can't do it... I could really do something if (someone or an organization) treated me better,* are like rudders on the ship of your life. You don't see the rudder and you don't see your shadow. You're barely familiar with your thoughts. And you don't see your neural pathways, either, because they're under the surface, steering your course. There may be hundreds of personal slights and beliefs that pass in and out of your thoughts, or that you speak quietly to yourself about, unaware of their impact. This was true for me, too, until I learned that some of those thoughts are actually lies. That's when I had to come to terms with myself.

Let's assume there's something in your life that you'd like to change, or that you're interested in becoming your greater purpose, in spite of your obstacles. A good place to start is the basics. To simplify a very complicated matter, imagine your life is a math equation:

$$(Ex + Em^x)F = D$$

On the surface, the equation looks complicated. The **Ex** are your experiences – the stories that made you. The **Em** are the emotions tied to those events. The exponent **x** is the intensity of that emotion, which amplifies the significance of the event. **F** is the frequency in which you experienced these stories, both highly emotional and less memorable. Finally, **D** is how you define yourself, others and the world at large. Because you've had many experiences, there are many things that you've defined. You have many **Ds**: how you view money and people, what you think is possible, how intelligent you think you are, your willingness to take risks, what you believe about your social status, etc. Put them all together and that is how you see yourself:

$$D + D + D + D = \text{Perception of Yourself}$$

We define ourselves by the intensity of the emotions associated with our experiences. We do this because that's actually how we develop. Our experiences are the things we point to and say: "That's why I do, or say, or act like that." Experiences are tangible. They're a mechanism for assigning blame.

Neurologically, we tend to cling to highly emotional events because those are the most memorable, and thereby assigned the greater power over us. Those are the events we choose to define us, even if it's an inaccurate definition – and it usually is. We define ourselves with emotional experiences because there's less resistance, thanks to the power of our neural pathways.

It's easy to say: "I'm this way because that's what my parents taught me, or what was reinforced in my upbringing." Even if you don't verbalize it, you can internally blame your parents or other caretaker for your inadequacies and weaknesses, because it's just too preposterous to imagine that you'd intentionally hurt or manipulate yourself or others, or have an ugly personality of your own accord. No, we need a scapegoat whenever our shadow escapes and causes chaos in our life. We need someone to place the blame on for our monstrous behavior. Looking back, we're okay with taking credit for childhood mistakes; that's an easy one: you were a kid; you didn't know better – that's the excuse. But, now that you've grown up, who do you blame? Yourself? No way! You're better than that. It's your abuser's fault that you don't trust others. It's your ex-girlfriend's fault that you're uncontrollably jealous. It's your dad's fault that you can't control your anger. It's the system's fault that you were born into poverty, and are still struggling financially. The equation above is how you define yourself, and it helps you put your beliefs into context.

But what if there were a different option? What if you rewrote the old equation?

Let's find a new solution. Let's erase the board and pretend, for just a moment, that all of the events in your life have equal value. The hard memories. The good memories. The daily minutiae that you don't even remember, and the events that transformed you overnight. Let's try this more simplified equation:

$$(Ex)T = Y$$

In this case, **Ex** is still your experience, **T** is time and the **Y** is You. In other words, you are your experiences. In an interview with Tom Bilyeu, neuroscientist David Eagleman said: "Who you are is the sum total of all the experiences you have ever had." Author B.J. Neblett said: *"We are the sum total of our experiences. Those experiences, be they positive or negative, make us the person we are at any given point in our lives. And, like a flowing river, those same experiences, and those yet to come, continue to influence and reshape the person we are and the person we become."*

This new equation obviously oversimplifies who you are. It excludes your personality and desires. It removes the intensity variable, both good and bad, leaving you with just you and your experiences. What you do with that is your call. Besides, what can you do now to change anything in the past, but learn to cope, forgive and grow?

By removing emotion from the equation, you are left to define yourself with nothing more than experiences. You are no longer what you believed in the past but, rather, the person you can now become. You are left with a unique person, who was born hardwired with a particular personality, quirks and gifts that are yet to be discovered. With this equation, you don't focus on emotions or sources of pain – these are behind you; in this equation, you focus on what is ahead. You can't fix the past. You can't even change the people who hurt you. And you can't go back in time to relive your happiest moments, either. All you can do with this equation is look at where you are right now, and decide if this is where you want to remain for the rest of your life.

If that simple equation leaves you feeling powerless, it's doing what it's supposed to. If you feel powerless by removing the blame factor, that's good. That's a good thing because, without someone or something to blame for your problems, or faults and poor habits, you will never begin to find your internal strength to move forward, to heal those scars, or let go of the crutch you've been using.

What crutch?

The crutch you've been leaning on are the stories you've allowed to define you. As long as you have that crutch, you'll perpetually lean on the past and your scars, as the reason for not reaching your full potential. Oh, you may not say that out loud, but you'll think about it every time. As a result, you may never take responsibility for your lack of progress or fulfilling your lifelong dreams. The downside of letting go of that crutch is that you'll immediately lose your balance. You see, the longer you've leaned on your emotional crutch, which grew out of past experiences, the longer you've neglected the muscles you need to grow into the person you were meant to become. This is literally what it means when someone says you're letting your past define you.

In his book, *Psychoanalysis and Repetition: Why Do We Keep Making The Same Mistakes*, Juan-David Nasio states: *"Our life beats to the rhythm of repetition that the unconscious impels. In the end, the unconscious is the force that pushes us to actively reproduce, from our earliest years, the same type of amorous attachments, and the same type of painful separations, that inevitably mark our affective lives. Thus, repetition is both healthy and unconscious: a life drive. But the unconscious is also the force that pushes us to compulsively reproduce the same failures, the same traumatic moments and the same pathological behavior. Thus, repetition is both pathological and unconscious: a death drive."* [3] With decades of psychoanalytic work under his belt, one of the founders of the Séminaires Psychanalytiques de Paris, and 1986 winner of the French Legion of Honor, Nasio's work focuses on how our minds drive us to repeat what it knows.

You see this in yourself, but maybe you don't think about it much. The known is safe. Familiarity, no matter how toxic, is how you navigate life, how your heart keeps beating and how you respond to most situations. You default to your physiological processes, and thoughts that have been repeated over and over.

If you don't believe you're living in the past, let me correct you, because to a certain degree we are all making decisions based on our past experiences. One example is an exercise I use in my mindset training. In this exercise, I have the audience stand up and give each other a high five, fist bump and elbow bump. The results are predictable and repeatable. The reason is simple: over the course of your life, you have given and received hundreds, if not thousands, of fist bumps and high fives. The purpose of that action was to encourage, motivate, develop teamwork, inspire and build confidence. Unbeknownst to the audience, I activated each individual's neural pathway that triggered those good feelings, by the sheer act of giving a high five. Author, speaker and podcast host Mel Robbins writes about the power of the high five in her book, *The High 5 Habit*, and demonstrates that giving yourself a high five in the mirror every morning can lift your spirits and motivate you, by initiating the high-five neural response, which is simply the physical movement and visual connection when you give yourself a high five.

By asking my audience to give each other a fist bump, I'm bringing their brains into the past and forcing them to respond according to what they learned when they were young. It works every time: everyone feels happy, is smiling and their mood is elevated. I encourage you to try giving your family, friends, coworkers and customers high fives and fist bumps on a regular basis, and see what happens. You can thank me later.

The high-five example is a microcosm of what living in your past looks like. Your brain responds to situations in the present by looking back on what it learned in the past. Your brain does not predict the future; your brain interprets the present only with what it knows from the past. Therefore, your mindset is simply a reflection of how your brain navigates the present with old information, regardless of what was real.

Another exercise I use is the apple test. In this experiment, I pretend to hand audience members an apple. With the room perfectly quiet, I ask them to imagine bringing the apple to their mouth and taking a bite. After physically performing that motion, I ask them if they could hear the crunch of the apple. The answer is almost always a resounding yes. This works because the motion of bringing an apple to your mouth and biting it is an action we have done over and over in the past. The experience of biting an apple is accompanied by the juicy, sweet flavor and the crunchy sound of our teeth breaking through the skin. Our brain recorded this experience possibly hundreds of times and, just like the high five, recreates the physiological, audio and emotional experience it learned many years ago. If you're really tuned in, your brain will add the sounds and maybe even cause you to salivate. You see, your brain, as complex as it is, loves familiarity, and will spit out the same data until new information is added to its pool of experiences. These are simply neural pathways replaying the past.

Dwelling on problems you had last year also keeps you in the past. Making fear-based decisions, because of something you experienced when you were a kid, is another way you live in the past. How you perceived the world when you were seven also replays in your mind today.

Alan Gordon, author of *The Way Out: A Revolutionary, Scientifically-Proven Approach To Healing Chronic Pain*, wrote: *"The truth about resilience is that it's a learned behavior. If you gravitate toward hopelessness, it's not because you're hopeless, but because your brain has done it so many times before. If your mind naturally goes to despair, it's not because your situation is dire, but because you have developed strong neural pathways for despair."*[4]

There are probably a thousand choices you instinctively make, every day, because of your neural pathways and habits. You don't spend much time thinking about your morning routine; you just wake up and go through the motions. And, even when you find yourself in a conflict, or struggling financially, or questioning your worth, your brain tackles those issues by reflecting on your past to determine a course of action. Unfortunately, we generally end up addressing our life issues with the same broken process or distorted perceptions. This is why so many people want more but end up back where they started, with an abusive guy, with a controlling girl, broke, hating their job, and so on.

This isn't true for everyone, though. Did you know that 1,700 people become self-made millionaires in the USA every day? It's important to know that only 3% of them inherited that money. According to the Ramsey Solutions National Study of Millionaires,[5] the vast majority built their wealth by having a winning mindset, which helped them overcome the same struggles most people deal with: low income, sorrow, illness, physical impairments, family problems, health and social disadvantages. Clearly, when you think something is out of reach, like a placebo, it will be out of reach. And, when you think an experience has meaning, you will find the meaning in it. And, when you have a sense of purpose in your life, you tend to be happier, healthier and wealthier.[6]

As you progress through this book, you'll discover why some people reach their full potential and others don't. Just look around. Many people struggle to rise above their circumstances. Common research shows that 75% of Americans lack a sense of purpose. Not only is there a noticeable gap in wealth between the top ten percent and everyone else, there's a large gap between those who reach their full potential and find meaning, as well.

If you find this interesting, welcome to your life. You, like many people, may want something different or better in the future, but you may be living in the past, subconsciously trusting your habits and thinking patterns to attain something that actually requires a different person, with better habits and new thought patterns. Solving this problem is the crux of this book: to help you get what you want, reach your full potential and become your greater purpose, by teaching you what it takes to leave the less capable you behind, and become the person capable of reaching your dreams.

Look, I'm not a doctor, or a psychologist, or a counselor. I'm just a guy who has had to deal with my issues and, after earnestly reflecting on who I am, where I came from and what I want, I realized that I was going about life in the wrong way – the wrong way for me, anyway. By some stroke of luck, I discovered the web of deception that I was living in shone a light on my fears and beliefs, which were simply incorrect, and I learned a new way of thinking; a better mindset. And that way of thinking has opened my eyes to a new reality, where I am incredibly free from the weight of what I thought defined who I was and where I was going. In doing so, I unleashed a wide-open prairie of possibilities, blooming with choices and options that I never imagined existed for me.

But how did I get here? What right do you and I have to unequivocally become whoever we want to become, or do whatever we want to do with our lives? Well, there's not a simple answer to that question, because life's complicated, no matter who you are. Like anyone else, my life has had its fair share of ups and downs, twists and turns, and so has yours. Am I right? You have stories that are painful, too. So, if you haven't come to terms with them, it's critical that you do so. If you need help, I urge you to seek professional guidance. If you know you're just hanging onto a crutch, free yourself and let go. Lose your balance. Fall down. Then get up and try again. This is your life. Don't let old memories reign over you any longer.

Now let's continue our journey together. But, before you move onto the next chapter, it's imperative that you take time to work through the chapter review, reinforce what you've learned and answer some really important questions. In the process, you'll begin to learn how your neural pathways are impacting your life, and what's possible if you replace them with new ideas and thinking habits.

Chapter review.

- What are the major takeaways for you in this chapter? How can you apply them to your life today?

- Are there experiences in your past that are still impacting your life choices? Can you see how those experiences are like a record, playing over and over, causing your past to dictate your future?

- How have those experiences impacted your confidence? Your potential?

- Think about the beliefs that influence your choices:
  - How do you perceive money? When faced with financial decisions, do you find ways to get what you want or settle for less, because your self-talk finds reasons for you not to get it?
  - How do you perceive yourself? When faced with an opportunity, do you talk yourself out of taking risks or stretching to reach a big goal? Be honest, how do you describe yourself when you're considering a challenging opportunity?
  - How do you perceive others? Do you think people who appear beautiful and have nice things, more money or esteemed positions are more deserving than you are?
  - Have you ever asked why others have a seemingly better life? Then, do you justify your lot in life by deciding that those rich people are probably unhappy, spoiled, privileged or greedy?
  - If you believe that everyone is equal, which they are, why then do you not deserve the same luxuries, or lifestyle, or freedom to get what you want from life?

Chapter 3

HOW EXPERIENCES BUILD

YOUR MINDSET

"No matter what you've experienced, remember this: there are people who've had it better than you and done worse. And there are people who've had it worse than you and done better."

John C. Maxwell

I literally grew up in a pink house, just like the John Cougar song, "Pink Houses". We lived on Kensington Drive in Saginaw, Michigan, a city that had a lot of racial tension but, at the same time, all of my childhood friends were diverse; lower middle-class, black, white, Italian, Latino, Protestant and Catholic. I remember what seemed like an army of kids playing freeze tag in our yard, hide-n-go-seek until the sun went down, basketball, "Olympics" and other yard games. Overall, I had mostly good memories there. I was the fourth-born child, until my parents had two more girls in the early 1980s. I suppose, like in any family, there may have been certain benefits to being the baby boy, but if there were, I didn't know it.

I lived on hand-me-downs, and had to start buying some of my own clothes when I was thirteen years old. My parents were religious, matter-of-fact, hard-working baby boomers. My mom is one hundred percent Polish and my dad is a mixed bag of English and otherwise European. There wasn't a lot of laughing in our family, like I had seen with other folks – especially my black friends; they laughed all the time. We rarely laughed together as a family, but we looked first-rate – on the outside, anyway. We went to church, wore clean clothes and got spanked when we deserved it. So, if that sounds normal, then I think that's what we were – as normal as I understood it, anyway. Dad put food on the table and did the heavy lifting, and mom did everything else. They were baby boomers through and through.

In 1975, we had a dog that had a habit of escaping. He was an Alaskan husky named Suka. Sounds like a cool name for a dog, but Suka means "bitch" in Polish, which is curiously perplexing, because my dad's stepmom would call my mother "that Polish bitch" when they were dating. I don't understand how that managed to become an acceptable name for our dog without causing immense pain to my mother, unless they just didn't know the definition of the word. Although, I have to plead ignorance, too, because I published a short story in a horror magazine, with the title, "Suka: The White Wolf", before I knew the Polish definition. Anyway, Suka was a great dog, from what I remember and, whenever I see an Alaskan husky, I get warm and fuzzy feelings, because I remember petting and feeding her.

We had gerbils, too. Unfortunately, I killed one of the gerbils with a Hot Wheels racetrack – you know, the orange tracks you connect with that little connector piece. I loved that track. You could lay it straight, curve it, loop it or just raise it up high, for a gravity-powered race. Yeah, I killed that poor gerbil with one of those. *Snap! Snap!* That sin haunts me to this very day. I pay that forward by feeding nuts to the squirrels in our local park, where I live. The squirrels don't think much of it, but it means the world to me.

We lived in Michigan until I was eight years old. Much of what I remember about living there is play and sibling interaction. When I was around five or six years old, I'd play so hard that sometimes I'd forget to take time to go to the bathroom, and had a lot of accidents, wetting myself frequently in front of my friends and siblings.

One day, I peed my pants again and my mother was furious. She had previously told me that if I peed my pants one more time, she was going to make me wear a diaper and put me outside, for everyone to see. And that's exactly what she did. After helping me get my wet, stinking clothes off, she wrapped me up in a cloth diaper, while I was kicking and screaming – which would've taken all the strength she could muster – she forced me out of the house. Understandably, I was kicking and screaming all the way across the threshold. Then she pushed me outside, locking both the front and side door – no shirt, no shoes, just me and that diaper. Obviously I was embarrassed, mad and crying hysterically. I don't know if my brothers were instructed to do so, but they gathered some of the neighbor kids to watch the drama unfold. I pounded on the door while the kids were laughing, but Mom didn't respond. At that point, my fight-or-flight instincts took over, and I went into the garage and grabbed one of the croquet mallets. Then, like a boss, I started beating on the door until she finally let me in; this little, war-torn soldier and his injured pride fell into my mother's arms, as she dragged me off the battlefield, into the safety of our little pink house.

This story illustrates one of the most painful moments that I can remember. We later found out that I just have a small bladder; nothing to do, nothing to fix. I'm still the one who needs to go to the bathroom all the time, whenever we're traveling. Our kids laugh and I get teased. I can't beat them with a croquet mallet, so I just exit the highway, laugh with them and do my business. But I can't escape the memory of getting locked out by my mother; it will always be there.

Stories like that can play over and over in your mind. You never forget them, nor should you. That story is real and raw, and impacted me in ways I may never know. Of course, that was many years ago and it no longer bothers me, nor do I feel any anger toward my mom. Over time, that story may have contributed to a sense of shame and anxiety, and formed a neural pathway designed to protect me from experiencing dread in the future – there's really no way to be certain, other than knowing that I became a very shy, insecure kid. When you're a bedwetter, you carry a lot of shame and feel dirty. That changed me, and my brain made adjustments to deal with it.

The world was changing in those days, too. We had recently come off the Vietnam war. Gerald Ford was the president. The Rubik's Cube was gaining popularity. Mood rings and bellbottoms were a thing. Eight-track cassettes were a hit. *Saturday Night Live* premiered. I was just a kid, so I didn't pay much attention to politics; what mattered was that our family sat together watching television every evening, like a nostalgic postcard, watching *Welcome Back, Kotter, Starsky and Hutch* and Disney, on Sunday evenings. We ate dinner together every day, hoping that we didn't eat too sloppily, or we would be forced to eat our food on the floor, "like a dog, if that's how you want to eat." Back then, kids didn't have to wear seatbelts in the car and you could stay outside all day, as long as you completed your chores and came home before the streetlights turned on; break those two rules and your life would end, swiftly and silently, with no record of your existence – at least, that's how I interpreted it in those days.

Funny how the threat of losing your life, or public humiliation, doesn't stop a kid from doing stupid stuff. Yeah, I did a lot of stupid stuff, like climbing a telephone pole and then falling on the chain-link fence below, apparently attempting to lobotomize myself. The lobotomy was an absolute failure, but I did come within a fraction of an inch of tearing my temple off my face. Yet another bloody mess I will never forget. In total, I would crack my skull four times over the years, leaving a trail of scars across my face that map my life story.

A couple of years later, during the 1978 blizzard, a friend and I made a unique friendship pact. We called ourselves "spit brothers", because we didn't like the idea of cutting ourselves to form a "blood pact", so we shared our spit – my spit in his mouth, his in mine – forming that endless and irrevocable bond known as spit brothers. You'll be glad to know that I only have one spit brother. Aside from slurping my friend's saliva, the blizzard was truly magnificent. After a couple of feet of snow fell, we got a covering of ice, and that's when things went from winter to wonderland. Everything was frozen. When I walked on the snow, I didn't fall through because the ice was really thick. This had a magical effect, because it coated everything with a sparkly shimmer. The chain-link fence in our yard was glassed over with ice, and it was so pretty to me that I remember dragging my little red wagon next to it, then beating the fence and watching the ice crystals fall into my wagon bed. I filled it up with crystal-clear water candies, which I enjoyed for what seemed like hours. We also had a willow tree in the back yard, which was so frozen over that the branches were weighted down to the ground, forming a beautiful ice castle. I pulled the frozen branches apart and walked inside the crystal temple, then sat in my willow-tree sanctuary, eating ice candy until my little fingers and toes couldn't take it anymore.

In the fifth grade, I got stabbed in the leg with a No.2 pencil, by my childhood nemesis Ronnie P. I don't know why he did that, but that sort of behavior wasn't unusual for him. We were always at each other's throats. What I can't understand is why our teacher would connect our desks, facing each other; makes no sense. And that's when he struck: when I was most vulnerable. Brilliant strategy: with the pencil secured in his shoelaces, he kicked his weapon forward and the pointed end went through my jeans, into my leg; I still have a black mark inside my skin, where the graphite penetrated my flesh. After grunting in pain, my teacher realized I was hurt and sent me to the nurse's office. The nurse tried to pull the sharpened tip out of my leg but, no matter how hard she tugged, it wouldn't budge. So, my mom took me to the doctor, where they had to perform a minor surgery to get it out. Oh, well, just another day at the office for me.

That same year, I pretended I was skiing down one of those wavy kid slides, bumped a little too high and went flying, hands first. Two of my fingers took the brunt of the inertia. If you want to understand the damage that was done, hold your left hand in front of you (palm facing away), then pull your ring and pinky fingers over the top of your middle finger and point them both down, toward the base of your thumb – that's how broke they were. Still makes my butt hurt thinking about it.

Let's not forget my sordid affair with cigarettes. And, to avoid any confusion, you should know that at this point in my life I was not aware that smoking killed Bookstore Grandpa. So, unfortunately, I smoked cigarettes from the third through seventh grade. I attribute the allure of the brown leaf to my father's vile habit. He was a chain smoker, from the time he was in high school until he was forty-years old, so there were always ashtrays and cigarette butts lying around. While he was away at work, I slowly developed the habit of sneaking his leftovers out of the house, straightening out what was left of the smashed butts, and smoking the cigs until all that remained was the filter. I felt like it was my personal responsibility to finish the job he couldn't complete. Ironically, the words I frequently heard my parents say – "Waste not, want not," – backfired, giving me permission to smoke at every chance I could. I preferred the Marlboro brand, because I felt like a rebel. I later graduated to smoking weed with my brother and our good friend Rich, when we played *Space Invaders* on his Atari system and ate popcorn, while his mother worked Saturdays at the factory. You don't forget smoking weed and playing Atari with your big brother; you never forget something that epic!

The award for the most traumatic stunt I remember, however, went to one of our neighbor friends, when he jumped off a high dive at this swimming hole we frequented in Ohio. We liked to play water tag, all around the L-shaped dock. The poles that supported the dock had these coned-shaped toppers, meant to provide a protective cover. Well, one day, while the kids were swimming and chasing each other, over and under the dock, the award-winning adolescent jumped off the high dive and landed a little too close to the pier, unfortunately catching his left nut on one of the poles which, by chance, was missing the protective cap. He lost his left nut that day, but the dock, the pole and his testicle are still there, to testify to the dangers of being unaware of your surroundings.

I didn't win any "idiot" trophies, but I did climb on top of my dad's convertible 1963 Ford Falcon. Yes, sir, I climbed right on top of that old bird – and just as quickly fell through the roof. I don't remember much after I walked inside our house; one of my siblings snitched on me and things sort of went black. Last thing I remember hearing was something to the effect of "gonna hurt me more than it's gonna hurt you."

You could call those events childish, silly or foolish mistakes, which we all make. They were foolish and embarrassing, and in some cases painful. And, over many years, those stories built the person that I thought I was: inadequate, dirty, less. Although I excused myself for my immature behavior, through most of my adulthood I held my parents and others to account for any emotional scars that I incurred – it didn't matter if there was another side of the story – meaning that I had plenty of grace for myself, but not much for anyone else. Now, looking back, I have a different view: I see each painful and embarrassing moment as beautiful. I see those experiences for what they are: my story.

My developmental journey is as unique as yours. Those stories have a special meaning, not only to me but to anyone who feels the way that I did: dirty, inadequate, small, aimless and insecure. Sharing those stories with you gives me an incredible sense of meaning, because I know that you have crazy and painful stories of your own. And your stories are building the person that you are, too. In fact, sharing your story with people who need to hear your experience is a great way to add meaning and purpose to your life, because there's always somebody who needs someone like you. Someone who relates. Someone to look up to. Someone who has overcome the same obstacles.

While growing up in that little, pink house, I barely knew anything about life. I was developing my self-concept, how I saw the world and how I viewed others. I was broadening my scope of trust and mistrust. I was learning if the world was a good or harmful place, if I was capable, and where I was going to fit into the big world around me. In my case, I believed people were scary. I was weak, I was fearful and I felt small among larger personalities. Was this my mother's fault? Was it the fault of my father's physical and emotional absence? Does it matter now? No, it does not. We are all broken. We are all becoming. We are all on equal footing. We are flesh and blood, heart and soul, and we all feel pain, in ways that are unique to our upbringing and personalities. That's what makes us so similar, in spite of our differences.

Like most people, I'm as capable of hurting others as anyone. I'm capable of saying nothing when I should speak up. I'm capable of making a bad choice that could destroy a life. I'm guilty of being self-absorbed. I'm guilty of telling lies. I'm guilty of letting my fears control me. I'm guilty of inflicting painful words. I'm guilty of a lot of things.

And so are you.

Read that again.

You're guilty of a lot of things. And so am I. We all are.

Of course, there are extreme circumstances, and we let family services and the courts sort those out, but how your parents raised you, and how you interpreted the world through your young eyes, is yours to hold onto, accept or release.

This is a reality you must come to grips with, in order to move forward. This is why your past must remain in the past. This is why you must forgive. This is why so many people let their past control them. If you can't believe that you have the capacity to hurt others – and it's likely that you have – then there's a chance that you're probably not taking an honest look at yourself. And it's so important to be self-transparent, in order to truly know who you are. Until you see yourself as equal with the rest of humanity, it will be difficult to forgive and to have empathy for others. If you can't move forward and forgive, you will be stuck back there until you can, and the program that you received will continue to play, repeating the same story, the same plot, the same ending.

So, what will you do? Will you dig in your heels and continue the cycle? Will you let your old mental habits define you? Or will you forgive and change?

The perceptions that were etched into our brains at a young age carry forward, in how we respond to any and all situations through our adulthood, for good or ill, unless we are otherwise made aware, experience some sort of intervention, or experience a crisis so severe that we're forced to change. And that's a crazy concept: that most grown-ups are walking around in adult bodies, making choices with the same general view of the world, and the same fears they had when they were children. It's sort of like raising a child in a movie theater and exposing the kid to horror movies, or Disney movies, or love stories, or action/adventure movies. If that's all you've ever known, that's how you will perceive the world, indefinitely, unless something changes. Unless you intentionally change.

The most impactful experiences of your life built a foundation for your mindset, and it's not uncommon to carry your parents' mindset with you, throughout your life, whether you're aware of it or not.

Don't confuse mindset with mood; waking up grumpy isn't a mindset problem. Your mental state and mood can change rather quickly, with something as simple as exercise, breathing, prayer, yoga, meditation, an ice bath or other methods. Your mindset, however, is formed when your early training and neural pathways converge with the environment, which you experience over and over and over. Your mindset is how you see yourself, others and the world at large. Your mindset is fluid and determines your choices, perceptions and the way you respond to life, based on what your mind is set upon. If your thoughts are fixed on negativity, your mindset will remain negative. If your thoughts are set upon growth and development, you will continuously improve in all areas of your life.

Examples of an unhealthy mindset can be negativity, constant criticism, belittling of others, fear of failure, the belief that your failures define you, or the belief that you cannot change. Examples of a positive mindset are when you look at each day as a wonderful gift; the belief that daily opportunities abound; the belief that people are generally good and want to be your friend; the belief that you can succeed if you put your heart into something, and that if you fail it only means you may need to learn something new or keep trying. That's called a growth mindset. The opposite of a growth mindset is a fixed mindset. If you have a fixed mindset, failure defines you and winning paralyzes you, because what if you can't do it again?

Like most things in life, there is a spectrum, where we can be far to the left or far to the right, and anywhere in between the two mindsets. *The point to remember is that, if your mindset is what your mind is set upon, then your mindset can be altered if you begin focusing on something different, something better, something more in the direction that you actually want to go.* I cannot emphasize this enough. This is a key component of mindset training, and it is why you must honestly evaluate how you're investing your mental energy.

Most of us have a variety of memories that trigger many of the genres I listed previously: action, horror, love, adventure, fantasy, comedy... And, having a great childhood, with wonderful parents, is a bonus, but that doesn't guarantee that you have a growth mindset and clarity for your life. In fact, if you had a healthy childhood and you still feel lost and aimless, you can wonder: *What's wrong with me?* The answer is that nothing is wrong with you; that's just how life works. It's mysterious.

Unlocking the mystery of your development is like trying to solve a puzzle with endless combinations determined by parental involvement: early bonding, childhood play and social interaction, father present or not present, intact family, siblings, birth order, geography, diet and so on. Yet, no matter what your combination, your early years formed thinking habits that have been repeated millions, if not billions of times over, until this very moment.

It's unfortunate that we don't talk about the concept of brain development broadly as a society, because the direction of our lives is often determined by that developmental process. Many people aren't aware of the significance of brain development, and how the process essentially forms the way they think as adults. Our brain continues to develop into our late teens/early twenties, until our prefrontal cortex is fully developed, as we (hopefully) begin making rational choices.

Unbeknownst to most of us, we are like moonshine soaking in oak barrels: the longer we marinate in our formative environment, the more we take on the characteristics and flavors of that barrel. The question on the mind of everyone who resents the barrel they were immersed in is how to turn whiskey back into water. I don't know if there's a good answer for extreme trauma, aside from lifelong mental care, love or a transformational experience with God, the universe, medical intervention, people who care, Jesus... it has to be significant intervention. And, even if you're not dealing with an extremely traumatic childhood, aren't you still left with questions? Why did they? How could they? Why didn't I? Why didn't someone stop it? Why do I do that? All the questions.

Your query can go on forever, in spite of any transformational or spiritual experience, because we were never promised all the answers. And that's the point. You can look back on your life and ask a thousand questions that will go unanswered. There may never be enough "right" answers to justify the pain, disappointments or emotional injury you experienced, because that is what life is: a trail of mistakes and errors in judgment that we all leave behind. It's important, however, to understand that what we've experienced is not the final answer. Who we are at this moment is only a snapshot. We are not static. We are fluid. We are becoming. So, the question is not: *who are you?* The question to ask yourself is: *who are you becoming?*

Please listen to this: the same whiskey barrel that made your particular concoction can be replaced when you start the process of distillation, the process of change. And that change starts with self-awareness and an honest look at yourself.

In the chapter review, dig into your mindset, how it was developed and what you really want from life. It's important to evaluate what brought you here, but it's more important to start thinking about where you want to go from this point forward.

Chapter review.

- What is your major takeaway from this chapter? How can you apply it to your life today?
- Take a few minutes to reflect on your life. Think about some of the major events that helped to develop your mindset.
- How has your mindset impacted the choices you have made over the course of your life?
- Does the world have to change for your mindset to improve?
- Knowing that the world won't change, what needs to change in you, to build a growth mindset?
- What do you want? This is a difficult question, and many people can't answer it without giving superficial answers, like a house, a new T.V., a new car or a better job. Sometimes we don't know what we want, because we don't know what we are capable of, and we don't know who we are. So, ask the question another way: if there were no limits on your capabilities, time and finances, then what would you want from life? For your career? For your family? For your health? For your finances?

Chapter 4

HOW YOUR STORY DEFINES YOU

"Humans are not mindless machines following a programmed script, but rather breathing beings with a yearning for meaning and self-direction. Without purpose, life becomes empty and dull."

Steven C. Hayes, Ph.D.

My love for music started when we were living in Michigan, because my parents had a fancy console and stacks of records. They had The Beatles, The Eagles, Sonny and Cher, Olivia Newton-John, Jim Croche, James Taylor and many more. You name it, they had it, and I would listen to anything playing on the turntable. To this very day, I have deep emotional connections that bridge my memories with music, and I'm grateful to my parents for bringing music into my life. It shouldn't come as a surprise that music became a big part of my life.

The summer after the blizzard, we moved to Aurora, Ohio. My love for music came with me. And so did the drama.

I started playing the drums in the fifth grade, rat-tat-tatting on the snare drum in our elementary school band. I spent an hour a day learning the basics, with a few other kids in my class. But I made my drum-set debut in the sixth grade, during recess. I found a little trap set in the band room and started beating on it – and, for the first time, I began dreaming that I was a rock star. The year was 1982, and there was a lot of good music at that time: Journey, Foreigner, Styx, Toto, Heart, Flock of Seagulls, The Go-Gos, Asia, The Steve Miller Band, Van Halen, Queen, Prince, Cyndi Lauper, WHAM, The Who, 38 Special, The J. Geils Band, The Rolling Stones, The Cars, Stray Cats, KISS, RUSH, The Police, The Cure, Talking Heads, Dexy's Midnight Runners... the list goes on and on.

By the sixth grade, the desire to play a drum set began to burn inside of me. With my trusty snare drum, I'd piece together plastic trash cans and laundry hampers, to complete the lineup. I'd play my little drum kit to Bruce Springsteen, Michael Stanley, Queen, Foreigner, Journey and the other bands listed above. When I discovered that paint cans could give me a wider range of tones, I added them to the mix, too. I later played with a group of friends from high school, for nearly ten years, and we won some contests, recorded an album and had a lot of fun. All in all, I've played rock, country, jazz, blues, and even played as Ringo Star in a Beatles tribute band.

My journey as a drummer was really one of my first experiences of feeling good about myself. Playing drums was fun, and a great way for me to burn off excess energy. It defined a good part of who I was, for many years. It was one of my first loves that loved me back. I was truly a drummer at heart, because I was tapping on everything long before I played on my makeshift drum set, and I'm still doing it to this very day. This much-needed confidence booster was a minor turning point in my life, but really began to take its full effect when I was twenty or twenty-one years of age.

In junior high and high school I was self-conscious about everything, like most kids. My self-esteem was very delicate, not only because my family life wasn't what I'd call a breeding ground for personal development, but also because I was a sensitive child to begin with. I was shy. I was unsure of myself. I was aimlessly trying to figure out where I fit in. However, that began to change when I hit my early twenties, when my band started playing more significant gigs: college parties, car shows and contests. Over time, I grew more confident with each little win. By the time we opened a concert for country singer Hal Ketchem, circa 1991, I was feeling pretty good about who I was as a drummer.

My middle-school art teacher, Mr. Kmetz, used to call me "Kinetic", because I was so hyperactive. Funny how he was able to appreciate that element of my personality, whereas my teachers and my parents would reprimand me for my inability to sit still, daydreaming and tapping on everything. Finally, a teacher recognized the value in a trait that later proved to be a talent – a gift that has brought joy to thousands of people, whom I entertained along with my teenage bandmates, blues players, worship teams and fellow Beatles tributaries, over the course of my life.

You have talents, too, and maybe more yet to be discovered. This would take me decades to understand. So, pay attention to your little wins and don't underappreciate the value you bring to the world. Be aware that you could be influencing others and never know what kind of difference you're making. You won't always get a parade in your honor, just because you impact a life. You don't have to turn the world on its head to inspire someone. If you want to become your greater purpose, it's important to believe that impacting one life is enough. You may never know if the small contributions you make are actually influencing anyone, and you don't need to know. Becoming your greater purpose will require pure motivations and humility. If you need to feed your ego, you're missing the point of a greater purpose.

As a freshman in high school, I could not conceive that I was valuable, or that I would ever contribute anything meaningful to the world. That's really a sad thought, but that's the God-honest truth. For the life of me, I couldn't see myself in the future. I know it sounds weird, but I tried to imagine who I'd be when I'd grow up and, every time I'd attempt prophesying five or more years ahead, there was nothing there. This was always a source of frustration for me, because many of my peers were already excelling in sports, math, science or leadership. When I was young, I didn't have any idea what I wanted to become. When I was in high school, I was frustrated by the pressure I felt to declare my "major" interest. I was clueless. I didn't know what the choices were. Business? Like I had any idea what that even entailed. Science? No way! Medicine? I was too dumb. Football? Basketball? LOL! I was 5'5", and 120 pounds soaking wet. I was timid. I was aimless.

Thankfully, a tiny sense of who I was began to emerge. Besides drumming, I developed a strong work ethic. As an adolescent, I would shovel snow, cut grass and deliver newspapers. In the process, I learned how to complete a task, no matter how hard it was. My parents made sure we did our chores and helped around the house. We didn't get an allowance; our chores were our responsibility, as a member of the family. So, kudos to Mom and Dad for making hard work a part of our culture!

Those lessons carried through into the eighth grade, where I started a little shoe-shining business at a local barbershop. My dad used to take us boys to get our haircut at The Carriage House and, somehow, I started cutting their grass and cleaning up the trash in the parking lot. I don't remember how I got that job but, not long after I started doing their yard work, I remember waiting to get paid by the barber, when I noticed all of the men were wearing nice shoes. My dad had a shoeshine set at home, so I imagined polishing the other men's shoes, like Dad did with his. I was a daydreamer; that's how I functioned. But that time I took action, and it was probably my first foray into entrepreneurship. Before I left for the day, I asked the barber if I could shine his customers' shoes while they got their hair cut. I'm not sure what he was thinking, although I bet he was impressed: thirteen-year-olds don't usually look for extra work. I remember him asking how much I'd charge, and I said that I didn't know. He said he'd think about it, and let me know what he decided the next time I'd come to clean the yard and cut the grass.

To my surprise, when I returned he had a plan in place. He said I could charge two dollars for shoes and three dollars for boots, plus tips if I get any, and he would supply the tools and materials. Then, he walked me back to his little storage room, where he had already mounted a set of shoe- and boot-holders to the wall. The barber said he'd charge me a couple of bucks a week to use the space, and then we shook hands, sealing the deal. I imagine he was more than happy to teach me some basic business principles. During this time, I had practically zero guidance in my life, in terms of anyone helping me discover my strengths, how I was wired and uncovering my gifts. Outside of my parents, I had two mentors who were making a positive impact on my life: Mr. Kmetz and the barber.

As a teen, I rarely felt confident in myself, regardless that others may have perceived me as a strong person. I can honestly say that I never remembered anyone suggesting I was confident, until maybe my junior year in high school, when I was voted class president. For the life of me, I didn't understand why they picked me, other than the fact that I was the new kid in town and no one had any dirt on me. I wasn't a leader. I wasn't seeking the role. I was a soft-spoken introvert, and this is generally still true today. I lacked confidence, mostly because of my bedwetting, home life and pants-peeing days, which lasted into the sixth grade. Yes, I peed my pants in the sixth grade, too. In public. In front of a class full of my peers and a nun.

I'll give you a second to stop laughing.

You okay? May I go on? Thank you.

Here's how my sixth-grade pants-peeing incident went down. It all started when I walked into CCD one Wednesday evening. What's CCD?

Good question! CCD is essentially the Catholic form of Sunday school, only we never went to CCD on Sunday. CCD stands for "Confraternity of Christian Doctrine", otherwise known as "catechism", otherwise known as the Catholic form of Christian education. Anyway, my parents dropped me off at CCD every Wednesday, after dinner, and I'd sit with a bunch of Catholic kids in a classroom, while a nun (we'll call her Sister Meanie-pants) taught sixth-grade catechism. Well, one day I had a very wet accident. It seemed as if my bladder would explode anytime it wanted to, and this day was no different. I had to pee about thirty minutes into the one-hour class, so I asked the nun if I could use the restroom. Instinctively to all meanie-pants, she said: "No, you can wait." And so I did, for another five minutes, but my little bladder started screaming for relief. I raised my hand again and received the same answer. Ten minutes later, I started looking for something close by that I could pee into, because I was getting desperate. If she'd say no, I'd feel obligated to obey; that's just how I functioned. With fifteen minutes remaining, I raised my hand a third time and begged her to let me go, but she refused. And then she upped the ante, and said that if I asked again, she'd send me to the Head Nun's office.

Now, at that point, most of you would have walked out of there after the first "no" and said: "To hell with this!" And that's my point: I was extremely timid and afraid of the big, wooden ruler on her desk. I was not a rulebreaker, even if it meant my own demise. So, I sat there, watching the second hand on the clock. *Tick-tock, tick-tock.* My legs were shaking. *Tick-tock.* My mind couldn't think of anything else. *Tick-tock.* My bladder was like a nuclear rocket counting down to liftoff, and it wasn't going to make it another ten minutes. *Tick-tock.* And it didn't. I sat there in silence, humiliated, as the urine slowly came out, no matter how hard I tried to keep it in. The warm fluid soaked into my jeans and probably puddled in my seat. I untucked my shirt to cover it up, and it worked for a time. But, when the class was over, everyone had to stand in line while we waited for the bell to ring. I stood last in line, as you can imagine. Still, I just couldn't hide it; one of the kids noticed my wet pants, and I'm sure he could smell it, too. Then, he pointed and said: "Eeeewwww, he peed his pants!"

I turned beet red and, although no one could see it, I was bawling like a baby on the inside. I vowed then and there to never go back. How could I? I would be the laughing stock of that class. The next week, my dad dropped me off, against my will, but he didn't know about me peeing my pants; I already had a history of bed-wetting, and I was not going to tell him what happened the previous week, for fear of being humiliated again. So, after he left, I walked right past the school and strolled around the neighborhood for an hour, thinking that I could just skip CCD. Nope! After nearly an hour had passed, I walked back to the parking lot, only to discover that Dad had been waiting there for several minutes, because the Head Nun called my parents and told them that I never showed up.

My situation was getting worse by the minute. Dad was pissed. My circumventing CCD was a direct assault against my mom and dad's spirituality. They were very Catholic, and this would look very bad. So, after he finished yelling at me, I think he finally asked why I didn't go to class. And that's when I started crying, confessing my sins: *Father, it has been a week since I last peed my pants. What is my penance?*

To my surprise, Dad walked me into the Catholic School to discuss this with the nun. I stood by his side, embarrassed, as would be expected, while he and Sister Meanie-Pants exchanged words. I don't know how that conversation went, but I never went back. They ended up sending me to a CCD class, affiliated with another Catholic church in a different town.

Another blow to my self-esteem occurred when I got straight Ds in the seventh grade. I wasn't a good student from fourth through sixth grade, but it couldn't have been more apparent in the seventh grade that

I was definitely a dummy. Although none of my teachers would have ever stated it quite like that, I believed it was true. And I almost got away with avoiding the problem because, for much of the year, my parents didn't even ask about my grades. Again, this was a very difficult time for my mom. Dad worked out of town for two to three weeks at a time, and mom had a lot on her mind. She was working at a nursing home, taking care of the needs of the elderly, while pregnant with her fifth child. So, having four kids to come home to, to fix their meals, clean house and deal with our immature bullshit, was more than she could handle at the time.

When I got straight Ds again, for some reason Mom asked to see my report card while it was hot off the press. Her eyes widened and I could see that she was disappointed; that was clear to me. I think she felt some sense of responsibility, and probably anger toward my dad, too, for not being present, and for leaving her alone for long periods of time. But the real blow happened when my older brother said something to the effect of: "What kind of idiot gets straight Ds?" Now, that cut me, especially coming from him, and those words have haunted me for years. They also burned a new desire in me to never feel stupid again. After many tears, I vowed to work harder and study, to learn my vocabulary words, actually read the assignments and do the worksheets – not because I was particularly bright, but the idea of being stupid was too painful for me to bear. I couldn't afford to fail at everything, and I was well on my way.

To put things into perspective, between the ages of nine through thirteen, I had been smoking weed, drinking beer or wine and smoking cigarettes, whenever said paraphernalia became available. I wasn't in a studious state of mind, to say the least. Those habits didn't make life any easier for me, and may have contributed to my stunt in growth; all the men in my family are at least 5'10", but I'm only 5'5". Studies have shown that childhood smoking can contribute to stunted growth. So, when you're already struggling to feel confident, being the shortest guy in the room doesn't help.

I wasn't good at sports during this time, for obvious reasons. The smoking started in the third grade, but the day I decided that I wasn't going to be stupid anymore, something clicked. Eventually, those bad habits started to fade away, not only because I wanted to change, but also because my older brother was getting involved in track and cross-country, and I wanted to follow in his footsteps. This began a turning point for me, but there were some obstacles that remained.

I have two older brothers, and I sensed that my parents looked at them as the good one (the oldest) and the bad one (the second-born son). The second-born was running away from our family life. One day, he got into a fight with our mother. He was definitely one of the sources of her stress – not because he was a bad kid, but rather because she didn't understand him, and she didn't know anything about child psychology. He was third in line, but the second-born son as it applies to birth order. He was a contrarian, and that didn't go over well in our strict Catholic home. But the real problem was when my mom called the cops, because some local punks were fighting next to our house. My brother went outside and told the kids what she had done, giving them a heads up. Mom didn't like that. Things heated up, and I'm sure they probably said some things that pissed each other off. They eventually barreled into our shared bedroom, screaming and getting physical. I felt really scared. I had never seen any of my sibs fight like that with my parents. But then it got really dark, when Mom started pulling his hair, shaking his head and yelling: "You're the devil! You're the devil! You're the devil!" I will never forget that moment, and I'm pretty sure it scarred my brother for life.

That was probably a turning point for him, too. Before long, running track became our escape. And we bonded even more as brothers with that common love. We both excelled at running, in light of our poor habits over the previous years. It took a few more years for me to blossom as a runner, although I don't think I was as good as I could have been; I lacked mileage, proper diet and form. But what I lacked in information was countered by my work ethic, and my desire to not fail, like I had done so many times before. I finally found a sport that I loved. Next to drumming, running defined me. I was fourteen and changing fast.

Looking back on that time, I've developed compassion for my mom, and dad, too. Mom was under so much stress. I always knew she grew up in an emotionally dysfunctional family, and had her own emotional wounds to deal with. So throw her pre-existing issues in with teens, babies, an emotionally absent husband, and it should come as no surprise that another web of generational dysfunction was spun. And, my dad's emotional and physical absence, coupled with his bitter-sweet personality didn't help either. As an adolescent, I wanted to spend time with him, and I enjoyed working on projects with him in our garage, but when I did it seemed as if those brief endearing moments were wrapped in a bow of painful, cutting words. When he was home, we had to walk on eggshells around him. He could be happy and playful in one moment, or bite your head off with his quick temper. But he, too, had his own demons from the past that he had to contend with. They both did. And yet, I love them dearly.

The power of a mentor

Later that year, I had another life-altering experience. I recollected this memory in 2022, while attending Toastmasters. I was in my second year at the club, working on improving my communication skills, when I needed to write a speech about mentorship. So, I thought about the mentors in my life and, *wham!* It hit me. Mr. Kmetz, the art teacher who gave me the nickname Kinetic. He was my favorite teacher in Ohio. Everyone loved him and, man, did he make a difference in my life.

I gave this speech in the 2023 Toastmasters International Contest, and won third place at the district level, which was a huge accomplishment for me. I wrote the speech to celebrate Mr. Kmetz's memory, and to raise awareness about the importance of mentorship, because this man was a saint.

Now that you know my story, you will understand why Mr. Kmetz is worthy of being remembered, and how critical he was in uplifting my self-esteem. This is just one story, however; Mr. Kmetz impacted my life in a dozen subtle, less dramatic ways, too. The following is the transcript of that speech:

"Have you ever had a deep, emotional connection between an experience and a song that you love? This is true for me, especially back in 1984, with songs like 'Purple Rain' by Prince, 'Time After Time' by Cyndi Lauper, and 'Wake Me Up Before You Go-Go'!

1984 is a year I will never forget, because of those connections, and because it was the year one of my mentors made a lifelong impact on me. It was also the year I played Dan in our school musical, 'Joseph and the Amazing Technicolor Dreamcoat'. Our director was the Incredible Mr. Kmetz. Mr. Kmetz was everyone's favorite teacher, because he listened and spoke to us with dignity.

It didn't matter what kind of monstrosity you made in his art class, he could find the beauty in it. He was encouraging and inspiring, and I needed that back then, because I was only fourteen years old. I wasn't a good student. I wasn't good at sports. I wasn't even growing anymore. I was, however, aimlessly trying to figure out where I fit in. By some stroke of luck, this short, pimple-faced kid got a role in the musical.

One day at practice, during a break, some of us snuck up to the second-story balcony in the gymnasium. If you think we were up to no good, or smoking something we shouldn't have, you would be wrong – on that occasion. Because, on that day, in 1984, we were breakdancing!

During that time, our marching band, of which I was a cymbal player, was raising money to play at Disney World. Sounds exciting, right? It was exciting – if you could afford it. I was stressed out. I needed to raise five hundred dollars. I worked odd jobs and weekends, and sold approximately four... hundred... million... oranges for the fundraiser.

Now, back to the balcony. There we were, breakdancing, battling it out, like all breakers do, and in walks Mr. Kmetz. He was furious! He shouted for everyone to 'Get out of here,' and we scattered. If Mr. Kmetz was angry, we must've done something reeeaaally bad.

Then I noticed that he was pointing. 'Everyone but you!' he said.

'Me?'

'Yes, you, Bennington! The rest of you, get back to practice!'

My legs were shaking. My heart was racing. I walked sheepishly toward him.

'Yes, Mr. Kmetz?'

'Don't worry, Jeff. You're not in trouble.'

'I'm not?'

'No. Look, Jeff, I know how hard you've been working to go to Florida, and I'm really proud of you.'

'You are?'

'Of course.   And I brought you something.'   Then he reached into his coat.   Like a magician pulling a rabbit from his pocket, he handed me a roll of twenty-dollar bills.

'Two hundred dollars should help you get there.'

I was dumbfounded.   Two hundred dollars?   On a teacher's salary?   After insisting that I keep the money, I told him, 'Thank you,' and gave him a grateful hug.

Then he shouted: 'Alright!   Recess is over, Bennington! Get back to practice.'

I hurried off and then he said: 'Hey, Bennington, one more thing: you're a good breakdancer.'   I went back to practice, happy as a lark... walking... on... air.

That's why I will never forget 1984: the music, the trip to Disney World, breakdancing with my friends, and that moment with the Incredible Mr. Kmetz.   It changed me.   It changed me because Mr. Kmetz taught me that a good mentor can impact a life forever.   He taught me that a good mentor will find that one thing you did right, when you thought you'd completely failed.   And he taught me that a good mentor will encourage you to soar to new heights.

Ladies and gentlemen, not only do we need mentors like Mr. Kmetz, we need people who genuinely care, the way he did, today more than ever!   Yes?   You see, Mr. Kmetz understood that there's beauty inside all of us.   Sometimes we just need someone to point it out.   And he knew that there are people all around, aimlessly trying to figure out where they fit in – like I was.

My challenge to you is to not only remember Mr. Kmetz, but to emulate his character by mentoring someone who needs it, by genuinely caring for others, and by giving sacrificially.   Because, if you do that, you could change a life!

And, in the process, change yourself. And, if you're really fortunate, and you love music and people, you just might create deep emotional connections that last a lifetime."

Turns out Mr. Kmetz retired after that school year, in 1985. He passed away in 2018, and will forever be remembered as one of the most beloved teachers in the history of the Aurora, Ohio school system.

After my freshman year in Aurora, I found out we were moving to Indiana. This would be one of several turning points in my life. The person I was becoming wasn't worthless, but I certainly felt like I was beneath most of my peers. I had defined myself internally as "less"; I felt less than the rich kids, less than the smart kids, less than the athletes and less than the kids who seemed to know where they were going. I'm sure this was a normal adolescent attitude, but I was very cognizant of those thoughts and it troubled me. The idea of moving to another state kindled a lot of fear and anxiety. I'm not proud of it but, the night before we moved, I got drunk, reaffirming how I felt about myself: less, dirty, dumb. I had no idea how long it would take for me to unwind what I believed about myself. At the time, I thought: *This is who I am. This is my future.*

Maybe you've felt the same way? Maybe you think it's impossible to change? Maybe you think your dreams are out of reach? If so, keep reading. I'm going to show you how you can change, and the laws that will help you along the way. For now, answer the chapter review questions – and remember to be honest with yourself. Knowing your backstory will help develop the person you are becoming.

Chapter review.

- What is your major takeaway from this chapter? How can you apply it to your life today?
- At your happiest moments, how did you define yourself?
- In your lowest moments, how did you define yourself?
- How have those contrasting beliefs developed in you today? How do you define yourself now?
- At the core of your being, what hobby or talent or experience gives you the greatest joy?
- How have those experiences developed the person you are today?
- If those things are still a part of your life, that's great! If they are not, what moved you away from the things that you enjoyed so much? Have your interests changed?
- Did you have a mentor that recognized your talents? How did they encourage you? What was your response?

Chapter 5

THE SCIENCE OF CHANGE

"There's talk on the street, it sounds so familiar.
Great expectations, everybody's watching you.
People you meet, they all seem to know you,
Even your old friends treat you like you're something new.
Johnny come lately,
The new kid in town.
Everybody loves you,
So don't let them down."

The Eagles

"The New Kid In Town", by The Eagles, became my mantra. Whenever I hear it today, I think of 1985.

The year my parents moved us to Greentown, Indiana, became a transformative period for me. Mom had two more baby girls, and my older siblings moved out on their own. My oldest sister got married when she was a college student, at Kent State University, my oldest brother got an apartment, and my brother right above me joined the Marines.

When we moved, I was the new kid in town, and I think some of my new friends assumed I was the oldest of three kids: me and my baby sisters. What they didn't know was that I had spent the first ten years of my life as the last born, and suddenly I had the responsibilities of a first-born. That really was a strange time in my life, but I began developing some interesting traits that helped me become a more well-rounded person.

It seemed as if my world had changed overnight. One minute our family felt out of control, with teenagers and babies everywhere, and the next minute Mom had one timid teen and two little girls. And babies were my mom's sweet spot; she was wonderful with my little sisters, but struggled with teens who had ideas of their own. We were a new family in a small, rural town, so the changes in culture were swift and drastic. Dad came home from work every day, Mom was less stressed and I was the new guy, who was a fast runner and a decent drummer. No longer a small fish in a big pond, I had been transported into a small pond. I felt like an imposter. Everyone was so nice, so welcoming and so Christian. Coming from Ohio, where I felt stupid (among many smart kids) and poor (among many rich kids), smoky and dirty (among many clean kids), it felt very strange to be viewed as a nice, smart, cute teen; completely the opposite of how I felt about myself! *Don't they know I'm stupid? I get straight Ds. Don't they know I smoke weed? I'll contaminate the youth group! Don't they know my brother is the devil?*

I was an imposter. I was not who they thought I was. And, I have to tell you, that false image of myself stuck with me for decades. How couldn't it? These were the messages and self-talk I had played over and over in my mind! By the time I was fifteen years old, the neural pathways that formed my image of myself, others and the world around me were pretty well fixed in place, and my mom and dad's relational dysfunction continued.

Later that year, I literally had a come-to-Jesus moment, but in spite of that spiritual transformation, inwardly and developmentally my self-image hadn't changed. Spiritually, I gained clarity, but I was still shy, soft-spoken and easily intimidated. Outwardly, things appeared to be much different.

I quickly became known as a good runner on the cross-country team, but hearing my name over the intercom, after doing well in a race the previous day, felt embarrassing. I needed the confidence booster, but for some reason I felt a sense of shame when everyone was looking at me after the announcements. I know that sounds weird, but that's how I felt. Before long, I earned a reputation as a good drummer, too. On the outside, I fit in. On the inside, I felt alone. I felt like I was late to the party, because many of my new friends had known each other most of their lives, and rehashed old stories that I weren't a part of. I was just the new kid in town. An exotic, imported forgery.

It should come as no surprise that kids can experience imposter syndrome, especially when you're the shiny new thing. Imposter syndrome is so extensive that, in an article by *Medical News Today*, up to 82% of workers and professionals are impacted; it can cause anxiety, depression, lack of self-confidence and shame.[7] Based on my experience, I have to say that sounds like most of my young adult life. For example, I graduated with a bachelor's degree from Indiana University, but for the longest time it felt illegitimate to me, because it took me eleven years and my degree was "only" in General Studies. Of course, today I feel differently. It took eleven years because I paid for it as I could afford it, and I worked and raised a family in the process. I also learned that a degree in General Studies is accepted in more graduate programs than many other degrees, because of the diverse education the graduates receive. In other words, I believed a self-imposed lie for many years.

Another reason I felt like an imposter as an adult is the fact that I earned a journeyman's status as a steamfitter/pipefitter, while working at Chrysler. But, for the longest time, I didn't feel like a "real" journeyman, because I trained in a brand-new plant, and the pipefitters who came from outside the UAW seemed to have worked much harder in their apprenticeships, and were more capable and knowledgeable in construction and blueprint-reading than I was. Looking back, I've realized that the trade is diverse, because tradesmen come from a variety of experiences; some are expert welders, some are better at installation and others are proficient in troubleshooting. After twenty years in the trade, I developed into an excellent troubleshooter. Another lie debunked.

The truth is, believing that we are small, weak or an imposter is not uncommon. And, like any lie we tell ourselves, we believe our self-talk because we trust the source. Are there lies about your past that you've believed? Is it possible that your perspective is impairing your progress? Is it possible that your perspective of yourself is what's keeping you from reaching your full potential?

We believe the messages we hear over and over. We fall prey to our neural pathways; we fall prey to our upbringing; we fall prey to our early programming, and it sticks with us into adulthood, unless something changes. Unless we put a stake in the ground and declare that our false and limiting beliefs are causing us harm, leaving us with a sense of worthlessness and/or insignificance. And, if you compound constant criticism from yourself, family members, a manager, or relationships that do not believe you have unlimited potential, you will only continue the charade, endlessly feeling lost, less, aimless, and living a life without purpose.

It's not only criticism from others that could be your problem; you could be the source of your own problems, too. Bad choices. Regret. Self-loathing. A mean-spirited personality. All of these forms of self-sabotage are nothing more than habits. These are behavioral and mental habits, designed to protect you from pain, but they're preventing the progress you desire. And they can be reversed. Again, if you are dealing with abuse, personality disorders or extreme habits, you may need to seek medical help.

You and you alone can change your life *if you want to.* That doesn't mean you have to stay anchored to an abusive person – oh, no, sometimes you have to walk (or run) away from a dangerous situation, for sure – but you do not need anyone else to change for your life to improve. You do not need your parents to change. You do not need the government to favor you. You do not need to move to another city. You do not need happier emotions. Why? Because you don't need them to change in order for your life to get better. And, even if other people in your life change, you still have the garbage in your head that needs to be removed. Only you can clean house. Only you have the power to rewrite your story by reprogramming your thoughts, which is probably the ultimate source of many of your problems.

People tend to stay where they feel most comfortable, and rarely take responsibility for changing. Many people believe that their lot in life is someone else's fault, so they wait for the other person to change – and, in fact, expect others to change, because they believe that's the only way their life will get better. This was true for me well into my forties, and this type of thinking nearly cost me my marriage. It's much easier to point a finger at a boss, institution, family member or significant other. Most people, without knowing it, are desperately clinging to their programming. And, even when their life is in shambles, they look outside of themselves for a fix. They hope they'll find love from someone new. They hope they'll feel more fulfilled in a better job. They hope others will change.

Your training, mindset and neural pathways have dictated your view of the world. And, as we discussed earlier, those beliefs were primarily established by the time you were seven or eight years old. This was true for me, too: I accepted the false beliefs that defined my mindset. Granted, I had some good characteristics and traits, as well, so I navigated what most would consider a normal, middle-class life: get a job, get married, start a family. Even so, I always felt like there was something more for me. I never knew what it was, but the idea of discovering "who I really am", or finding a purpose in life that aligned with my authentic self, seemed inexplicably unattainable.

My wife later described this constant searching as "the chase"; I was chasing after something, but I didn't know what it was. Career? Money? Knowledge? I lost myself in the chase. I didn't know that I was searching for meaning. I didn't know that was an option.

You, too, may be on a chase to nowhere. Maybe what you're searching for is a greater purpose, something that will give you meaning and fill that inexplicable void. If this sounds familiar, you must decide if you want to live in the future or continue living in the past, by repeating the same thoughts, all of which determine your current choices and mindset. This control mechanism is automated and predictable. The program will continue running if you let it. It's not difficult to understand. These are simply neural connections that have been trained, over time, to do what they're told. As complicated as it may seem, your brain is only making sense of the world that you live in: what it sees, hears, tastes, feels and thinks. Therefore, you have the power to hit a hard stop, if you wish, and begin editing what it sees, hears, tastes, feels and thinks from this point forward.

Not everything has to go. You can redesign your program and create a new framework for life, keeping what you love and the things you're passionate about, and unplugging the parts of the program that are undermining you from getting what you want. I have done it, and many other people have, too, some intentionally and some intuitively. Some of us needed help. Some needed to learn hard lessons. Some just need a little encouragement. I needed all of the above.

In order to understand how and when I learned that a new program was needed, I'll fast-forward to 2006, because that's when things really started to change for me. That's when I began the process of understanding that I must change, that I'm the weak link, that the only person "holding me back" was myself. This was a cataclysmic switch in the way I used to think, because the mindset I was taught as a child was a poverty mindset, a fixed mindset, and an external locus of control. And you can't turn that ship on a dime. It's a process that didn't fully come to fruition until 2020, another fourteen years later. In truth, the process will never be complete but, after changing the way I see myself, others and the world around me, I finally have a sense of peace about who I am, where I'm going and exactly what my greater purpose is. This wouldn't be possible if I hadn't taken drastic measures. This wouldn't be possible if I hadn't declared war on my old mindset. For over forty years of my life, that lost little boy was still searching for meaning, still pointing fingers, still afraid, still timid, still aimless. Until I learned that, if I change, everything will change.

Time to change.

I accidentally brainwashed myself circa 2008, but not in a good way. YouTube had taken me by storm, and I was diving head-first into the deep ocean of ideas that were becoming readily available; new ideas, alternative news outlets and videos from every corner of the world were pouring into my life, through YouTube, and I was swept up in it. Bigfoot, lost civilizations, ancient aliens and conspiracy theories of every flavor caught my attention. In less than a year, I was completely consumed with videos and conspiracy theories about the Bilderberg Group, Freemasons, the Illuminati, and Skull and Bones. I became a different person; I became irritable, distrusting, paranoid, less hopeful and less enjoyable to be around. The more I'd ruminate over these conspiracies, as true or untrue as they may be, the more my world began to darken. I essentially changed my persona from upbeat to hopeless and gloomy.

My thoughts were so transformed and intense that my first work of fiction, *Killing the Giants*, sprung from that wellspring of dark concepts.

That's right, I brainwashed myself to the point that my creative mind, inundated with speculative ideas of the powers that be, sprouted into a novel.

The consequences of this played out in nearly losing my marriage and freaking out my boys, by telling them that the New World Order was going to take over the United States, and tanks would soon be rolling down the streets of our small town. That's how bad of shape I was in. That's what self-imposed brainwashing looks like. That's the picture of me fully immersing myself in a story I wanted to believe.

That was my first experience of transforming my thoughts and beliefs, even though I didn't know I was doing it at the time. It took a couple of years before I realized I had literally indoctrinated myself. This was no different than propaganda and ideological architecture changing what I believed. And yet, isn't this what we do to ourselves every day? In our social media culture, we spend hours upon hours watching short, dopamine-inducing videos about cats, sports, and everything except what we want. Your self-talk reinforces what you believe, even when it's incorrect. You see, when you immerse yourself in something, you become that which you are immersed in.

In one of his training sessions, Dave Ramsey said: "How do you become what you think about? You do it on such a consistent basis that it changes the makeup and shape of your psyche, your spirit, your future and your destiny."

Whether conscious or subconscious, we tell ourselves all sorts of messages that build on and sustain our familiar programming, or other messages that feel comfortable. Thoughts like: *I'm ugly. I'm such an idiot. I can't do that. I'll never be rich. Risk is dangerous. You can't be too careful. I'm not smart enough. I'm not* _____ *enough.*

In retrospect, it was so easy to brainwash myself. And, if you're caught up in social media, interpersonal drama, Netflix-binging and negative self-talk, you're doing it, too. My interest in conspiracy theories, combined with my full immersion, quickly and easily took over my emotions and perceptions of the world and global leadership. Conspiracies were all I wanted to talk about. I had become my very own Joseph Goebbels, indoctrinating myself. Is this what I wanted? No. Is this what was happening? Yes!

Later, when I realized what I had done, I understood that, if I could transform my thoughts and attitude in such a negative way, I could do the same thing in a positive manner. And that's when I began watching TED talks, reading books and listening to speakers that would propagandize me in the direction I actually wanted to go, like toward better relationships, more joy, success, and gaining skills that would make me capable of reaching my goals and living a life of purpose.

When I learned that, by changing what I think about, I can create a new perspective on life, I decided to rewire my brain yet again. I started immersing myself in what I wanted, and began creating new thoughts and neural habits through repetition, visualization, emotion and action. *Wow,* I thought, *this works fast.*

That didn't happen until I asked myself what I actually wanted from life. When I gained clarity in what I wanted, I knew exactly what I needed to believe about myself, and where to immerse my thoughts. The more intense the immersion, the faster the progress. It doesn't matter if you want to get a black belt in jiu-jitsu, learn to fly, write a book or become a certified computer programmer, the deep immersion mentality can accelerate your vision when you're passionate about where you're going.

If you're alarmed at the idea of brainwashing yourself, don't get too excited; you've been doing it your entire life. We all have. Sports fanatics watch so many sports that it's all they talk about. Super fans of *Friends, Seinfeld, Stranger Things* or *The Kardashians* talk about their favorite shows ad nauseam. And we have other obsessions, too. Marathon runners obsess. Gamers obsess. Triathletes obsess.

Entrepreneurs obsess. But these obsessions are what make us proficient, build confidence, and develop meaning and purpose, when these are the things we want.

The point is that many of your obsessions are distracting you from getting what you really want from life. Therefore, I'm suggesting that you obsess over what you actually want, instead of complaining that you can never get it. I'm suggesting that, if you want to become your greater purpose, you will need clarity in your vision, and then you will need to evaluate what you are immersing yourself in, because you may be filling your time and your energy and your thoughts with distractions that are in direct opposition to your desires. And, when you haven't addressed your mindset, and you're diverting your attention, accomplishing your goals can be extremely challenging. This can be very frustrating, but it's frequently a self-induced frustration, that can be eliminated by shifting your focus.

If you feel like your vision is in line with what you want, then you are well above the curve. You're trending in the right direction; you may not have to reprogram yourself. You may need to get a little more focused, however, if you've believed the lies about yourself for a long period of time. If that is the case, you may have a little more work to do. You may require more self-propaganda – which, by the way, is simply a process of reinforcing thoughts and beliefs about yourself, over and over, with intentional repetition. This process is nothing more than creating new pathways, beliefs, or brain habits that support what you want out of life.

You are unique. Therefore, you'll have a unique path to figuring out your greater purpose, and your path will require change and effort. But, don't start with deep immersion; start by addressing your mindset first. The change process begins with addressing your mindset, now that you understand how powerful your neural pathways are. Once you've corrected or adjusted your mindset, you can then begin immersing yourself in the things you want, but you need a growth mindset for it to come together and work in your favor. Without a growth mindset, your immersion can backfire.

So, let's get into the change process. Let's talk about the science of changing your mindset and beliefs. Is it really possible? Can you change your mindset and overcome those old neural connections? What does science say about this phenomenon? Let's find out!

The science of change.

The first book that opened my eyes to how my mindset impacts my life was *Mindset: The New Psychology of Success*, by Carol S. Dweck, Ph.D. After twenty years of research, Carol had proven that we can fundamentally change our life by transforming our mindset, from a fixed mindset to a growth mindset. This had huge implications for me because, after reading Dweck's book, I knew that I had many of the traits associated with a fixed mindset. Her research gave me hope that I didn't have to repeat my family cycle, and that I can change how I view the world.

In her TED talk, Dweck explained that underperforming students in the most underserved schools, like those in Harlem, South Bronx and a Native American reservation, completely reversed their performance from the lowest ranking to the top, simply by changing their environment from a FIXED mindset culture to a GROWTH mindset culture. With the power of *YET*, the kids began to look at themselves completely differently, learning that if they haven't achieved something *yet*, it is still possible, contrary to the previous training which painted life (and the student) as good or bad, smart or dumb, if the objective was not achieved after the first try.

This is true for children, but can adults change their mindset?

Absolutely! The same process to change your mindset and belief in what's possible requires you to understand that intelligence and mindset can be developed. Dweck cites the beliefs you'll need to internalize, to make that happen [8]:

1. Embrace challenges.
2. Persist in the face of setbacks.
3. See effort to the path of mastery, with help and support from others.
4. Learn from criticism.
5. Find lessons and inspiration from the success of others.

According to Dweck, you can reach a "higher level of achievement" and a "greater sense of free will" when you break away from a fixed mindset, develop a growth mindset and take these five beliefs to heart. Imagine how a belief system like this could change your life. Imagine how this could change how you parent your children. Imagine what could happen to your business if you stop rewarding a fixed mindset, and instead reward your employees for building on those five core beliefs.

No matter how hard it is to stop your old way of thinking, if you want to kill a fixed mindset, you have to change your mental habits. You have to create new pathways, where your thoughts can break free from the ruts carved over time. Essentially, you create new neural pathways, like you did when you were a child. And in time, if you abandon your poor neural habits, they will fall off the branch and be replaced by the new habits you create. This is called pruning.

So, what's the secret sauce? How do you change your mindset? You must change the way you think; thinking is the key. Thinking is the secret recipe. It took me decades, but I discovered that I needed to change the way I think about myself, about others and what's possible.

The answer is simple but the process is difficult. If you want to become your greater purpose, you must understand how important it is to take control of your thoughts.

Brian Tracey said: "You become what you think about most of the time." And this idea has been repeated throughout history. The Buddha said: "Our life is shaped by our mind; we become what we think." The Bible tells us, in *Proverbs 4:23*: *"Be careful how you think; your life is shaped by your thoughts."* And Ralph Waldo Emerson said: "You become what you think about all day long."

The idea that we become what we think about isn't new. If you brood over crime most of the time, there's a pretty good chance you'll become a criminal. If you study science most of the time, there's a good chance you'll become a scientist. Thinking is the spark. A single thought, followed by intentional action, will set your dreams into motion. Once you start the process of thinking differently, there is very little effort needed for those thoughts to become a part of your life. The more action you take to kindle that spark, the bigger the flame.

If you're on a journey to become your greater purpose, and your old way of thinking is not serving you, you have to change the way you think. You have to rewrite the old program. You have to start believing something new, like believing that you have unlimited potential, or believing that you're capable of accomplishing anything you set your mind to, or believing that you are made for a unique purpose. It's not easy and it takes time, but it's possible. And, it's possible to change the way you view yourself, the way you view others and the way you view the world around you. It's essential that you do so, because if you've felt the way I have – aimless, less and without purpose – you could be there because of your beliefs and perceptions, *not because it's true.* You could be there because of false beliefs. You could be there because those false beliefs are grounded in neural pathways and a mindset that has never been challenged.

Well, it's time to begin challenging those beliefs.

It's time to lovingly reshape the lenses in which you see the world.

It's time to resist the matrix of ideas that were planted in you and download a new program – a program that inspires and encourages, and seeks out your greater purpose. Your beliefs matter. Your thoughts matter. The way you see the world matters. Your beliefs, thoughts and mindset impact your choices, destination and results. And, whatever you think is possible for you will dictate the effectiveness of your mindset training, too. In the words of Henry Ford: "Whether you think you can or think you can't, you're right." So, if you think this is a bunch of psychobabble, then that's what it will be for you. But, if you believe that mindset training, personal development and improved habits can change your life, they will.

Andrew Huberman had an incredible interview with Dr. Alia Crum, Associate Professor of Psychology at Stanford University, and Director of the Stanford Mind and Body Lab. In the interview, Dr. Crum shines a light on the power of mindset, and how it dictates results in exercise, diet and stress. Through extensive studies, she found that the power of your beliefs can actually impact the extent to which you become healthy. Ultimately, it's not just about what you eat and the type of exercise you do, but the results are also impacted by how you think about those habits, and how much (or little) you think they will benefit.

This was played out in Dr. Crum's study of hotel workers. In the study, she found that hotel workers were very active cleaning, changing sheets, walking and pushing heavy carts all day, but they didn't believe that they were getting any exercise. As part of the study, some of the workers were told that they were getting very beneficial exercise, which was true, and over a period of time, their health actually improved significantly. Their systolic blood pressure improved by ten percent, they lost weight, and they felt better about themselves and their work.

If our thoughts actually impact our results in health and wellness, are they impacting how we view our daily lives, work, relationships and finances, too? Absolutely! Thinking, *I'm always broke,* will only guide your subconscious to steer you in that direction. It's a simple formula: your thoughts steer your life. Therefore, we need to intentionally think about what we want: health, happiness, fitness, relationships, wealth, fulfillment, etc. Thinking makes all the difference. But how we think about these things also impacts the results.

Unfortunately, thought habits will not self-correct overnight. This is why changing the way we think takes intentional effort. If repetition established your old mindset, repetition can create a new one. The implications of Carol Dweck's studies show that we can change our mindset in a short period of time. Crum's study shows that, if you begin with a positive outlook, you are likely to see better results. Combining these two beliefs will help you more effectively create new neural habits that serve you, and replace the habits that have obstructed you from getting what you want.

Dweck's research further demonstrates that students who were praised for their effort toward a goal (growth mindset) chose to take more challenging tests, while the students who were praised for being smart (fixed mindset) chose the least challenging options, because once they accepted the role of being smart, they needed to protect that self-concept going forward, by limiting their risk. This is a big deal. And, I believe that many adults are still protecting their false self-concepts, by limiting what they choose to pursue. The implications of Dweck's work, when applied to your choices – career, mate, education and goals – are immense. The implications to employers are equally significant, particularly in regard to culture, and how they reward effort and hire new employees. Clearly, one group can develop a culture of growth, curiosity and learning, and the other can discourage personal development, risk-taking and ownership. We do this in our personal life and we do it in our businesses.

Take a moment and consider how many risks you've avoided because of your mindset. Those risks, if taken, could have drastically changed or improved your life. But, if you were afraid to fail, or chose otherwise because you couldn't face rejection, your life today reflects those decisions, as well. And there are many other ways that your mindset impacts your results. If you think that your possibilities are fixed, you have limited your potential. If you think that money is scarce, you have limited your financial possibilities. If you're not interested in learning how to improve your diet, how to have better relationships, how to improve your skills and how to make better use of your time, your mindset is the thing that could be "keeping you down". If you think you can't make more money because your boss won't give you a raise, or you're not cut out for college because you're not a "good" student, your mindset could be what's limiting your potential, not other people; not the system.

Think of all the things you've wanted to accomplish, and begin asking yourself why you chose not to go for it or, if you tried, why you quit. Honesty is the key; it's critical to take an honest look at yourself, to determine what kind of mindset you're working with presently. To do this, let's evaluate where you fit on the scale between a *FIXED* and a *GROWTH* mindset. One way to do this is to think about how you respond to some of the following questions.

EVALUATE YOUR MINDSET:

From what you just learned about fixed and growth mindset, where do you think you fit on the scale, with FIXED on the far left and GROWTH on the far right?

FIXED ←------------------------------------> GROWTH

Now answer the following questions:

1. When faced with a choice to purchase an item or experience that could enhance your life, or the life of a loved one, and you currently don't have the money to buy it, how would you tend to answer?
   a. We can't afford it.
   b. How can we afford it?

2. How do you feel about your personal development?
   a. I have limitations based on my past experiences.
   b. With effort and learning from mistakes, I'll accomplish my goal over time.

3. How do you think about perfectionism?
   a. Not everything has to be perfect, as long as I do my best.
   b. If I don't get things done perfectly, what's the point?

4. How do you respond when you try to reach a goal and receive criticism?
   a. I get defensive because I feel like I have to protect my self-esteem.
   b. I listen to what they have to say, in case there's something I can learn.

Your mindset impacts the results in every area of your life, and we're all impacted differently. Some lean heavily on a fixed mindset, while others lean more on a growth mindset, but there is a plethora of combinations. There are no rules that state everyone has either a fixed or a growth mindset. I suppose people can function with a growth mindset in some areas of their life, and a fixed mindset in other areas.

But, let's look at the way you responded to those questions. If you responded *b, b, a, b,* you could have a growth mindset. That's great! That means you're eager to learn from your mistakes and willing to try new things, even if the results are unpredictable. If you responded *a, a, b, a,* you could have a fixed mindset. Having a fixed mindset will undermine your desire for getting what you want and becoming your greater purpose. This isn't rocket science, but these questions can tend to reveal your mindset in general.

What's important to understand is that it's better to have a growth mindset if you want to reach your full potential, get what you want and become your greater purpose. And it's really important to understand that you can change. You can build a growth mindset, even if you tested one hundred percent fixed. ***You can change. You are not fixed.*** Remember, your mindset is only based on your original programming, and you absolutely have the power to reprogram how you think.

If you're tempted to get upset about who is to blame for your fixed mindset, I would urge you not to do it. Having a fixed mindset can definitely be determined by your parents' or other influencer's transference of their mindset onto you, but that's not always the case. You have the power to nurture whatever mindset you desire, and sometimes you nurture thoughts that work against you.

Does it really matter if you were taught to have a fixed mindset, anyway? No, it doesn't matter, because you're not looking back anymore. You're looking forward, because you now have the power to change. Now you know that a growth mindset can help you get what you want and become your greater purpose, you can begin the process of changing today. You do this by choosing (from this point forward) to question your thoughts and how you respond, and hold yourself accountable, responding to life with a growth mindset. By challenging yourself, and keeping Dweck's five truths at the forefront of your thoughts, you can change your mindset. To do this, I suggest writing the five truths on paper and reading them every day. Apply them to the circumstances in your life until they begin to sink in. Thinking about these ideas, verbalizing and applying them daily, by making different choices and taking action, will build a growth mindset in the same way that exercise takes time before you see results.

A practical application looks something like this: you've desired to start jogging, to improve your health, but you regularly get frustrated because you feel beat up and exhausted, and previously thought, *I'm not cut out for this,* so you quit. Now that you're building a growth mindset, and you're learning that *effort is a path to mastery* and that *you persist in the face of setbacks,* you wake up, read the truths you are committed to upholding, and try again. It'll be difficult, but *you embrace challenges,* so that, in spite of the struggle, you do it because you are focused on getting what you want. You haven't got this yet, but *with effort and repetition,* your body will respond. Don't overdo it. Walk more and jog less. Don't give up. Repetition is the key to developing a new habit and a new you. Break out of the fixed mindset. Think differently about what's possible for you, and you will see different results.

If you want to change your life, I recommend taking the 30-day mindset challenge. Not only will you acquire the tools to develop a growth mindset, the #30daymindsetchallenge will propel you into a lifestyle that will map out and steer you toward the life you desire. You can find the details on how to get started at the end of this book.

Locus of control.

There's another aspect of our thoughts that can undermine or strengthen our mindset. It's called our "locus of control". Locus of control is the degree to which you believe you have control over your life, choices and results. If you have an internal locus of control, you believe that you have the power to create the life you want by taking control of your choices, actions and results. If you have an external locus of control, you believe that others have this power. Someone with an external locus of control is caught in a trap of perpetual victimhood. All their problems are the result of what someone else did, what someone else said, or what some institution has done to keep them from reaching their full potential.

Your locus of control is an important aspect of your mindset, and it must be mastered. If you want more from life, you cannot give anyone or any institution power over you. That's not to say that people won't try to discourage you, or that you won't face obstacles, but you cannot realize your full potential if you think others control your life, choices and results. On the other hand, you can't plow through life like a steamroller, with a self-centered attitude either; you'll only destroy relationships if that's your approach. You need people in your life, mentors and folks to help you become your greater purpose. A growth mindset and internal locus of control will provide the healthy balance that's required for you to become your best.

You conquer your locus of control in the same manner you conquer your mindset: by becoming self-aware of your thoughts; by questioning your decisions and motivations, and constantly working to prune the thoughts that try to steer you back to an external locus of control. You have the power to change the way you think – you always have. And, now that you understand the growth mindset and internal locus of control, you have the power to change. You are the only one who can change the things that actually matter, and will actually make a difference in your destiny.

A practical way to begin changing is to write *"GROWTH MINDSET and INTERNAL LOCUS OF CONTROL"* at the top of a piece of paper. Underneath those words, write something like the following and read it every day; begin to internalize every word. Print and hang it where you'll see and read it daily, like on your mirror, in your locker, in your wallet on the dashboard of your car, etc.:

GROWTH MINDSET and INTERNAL LOCUS OF CONTROL

"I can grow and expand the person I am becoming. I can courageously learn and try new things. I have unlimited potential if I work hard, and commit myself over time. Failure is an opportunity to learn and get better. If I make mistakes, that's okay; I can improve with effort and repetition. I have the power to improve my life. I am in control of my life, choices, actions and results."

If you really want to change, and you're committed to building a better mindset, read this every day and begin taking actions that make these statements true. Don't just repeat the words, but learn and try new things. Work hard at this and commit. Recognize when you fail and have patience with yourself. Don't beat yourself up. If you fail at something, ask yourself what you can learn from your mistake. At the end of the day, read it again. Do this over and over, and you will begin to actively create new neural pathways. And, when you experience a win, your positive emotions will reinforce the new belief of what's possible, and the mindset that made it happen.

Writing and reading messages like that will begin the process of change and creating new neural habits. With time, effort and repetition, you will see remarkable results, especially when you put those thoughts into practical situations in your life, where you conquer your old mindset and defeat your old locus of control. When that happens, celebrate and reward yourself, because anytime you succeed you will want to do it again. And that's how new habits are born.

You can't change the past, but you can change from this point forward. The implications of becoming a better you can be life-changing. According to Dweck, a mindset can change within a year or less. And research shows that you will perform at whatever level you believe you can perform at. Dweck's research further implies that you can create meaning and purpose in whatever you choose.

In an article by Stanford University's Wu Tsai Neuroscientists' Institute, we learn how we can believe a story that's not true:

> *"'It's really important to understand we're not seeing reality,' says neuroscientist Patrick Cavanagh, a research professor at Dartmouth College and a senior fellow at Glendon College, in Canada. 'We're seeing a story that's being created for us.' Most of the time, the story our brain generates matches the real, physical world – but not always. Our brains also unconsciously bend our perception of reality to meet our desires or expectations. And they fill in gaps using our past experiences."*[9]

This is why it's so important to get to the truth. You may be successful and capable, and yet you could believe you're a professional imposter. You might be shy, and believe that you're not as valuable as the louder personality in the room, but your perceptions can be incorrect, biased by the mindset experientially passed on to you by your early influencers.

Today, we know that our brains are actually plastic, which means our brain is capable of changing with new experiences. Therefore, science has concluded that you can absolutely rewrite your mental program through experiential repetition. And I know this to be true, because I have been doing it for many years now.

In an article published in *The National Library of Medicine*, dated August 1, 2018, we learn that:

"For a long time, it has been assumed that brain plasticity peaks at a young age and then gradually decreases as one gets older. This is also underscored by the expression that one cannot teach an old dog new tricks, implying that people who have become used to doing things in a particular way will not easily abandon their habits and change their behavior. Interestingly, thanks to tremendous advances in medical imaging techniques for assessment of brain structure and function, mounting evidence for lifelong brain plasticity has been generated over the past years.

Practice leads to improvement in and refinement of performance on motor – or any other tasks – and this dynamic behavioral process is associated with altered brain activity, occurring in a similar manner in young and older adults. Besides functional brain changes, practice also induces structural changes, such as alterations in regional brain gray and white matter structures, that are typically recruited during task performance." [10]

Why is this important? It's important because too often we like to use the "old dog" excuse for not changing. But that's a myth. It's just an excuse. When we resist changing our mindset, it's more stubbornness than anything, which is a fixed mindset. There is truth that changing our thought habits may take longer when we're older, but it can be done. The more eager you are, the easier it is to change. If you desire to become the new and improved version of yourself, that desire will be your superpower. Believing you can change is the fertilizer that will nurture your growth.

Now, if you are dealing with serious issues, such as an uncontrollable temper, or other serious conditions, such as severe depression, you may need professional help. If that's the case, these techniques may not be enough. But they may help, and it can't hurt to become more self-aware of your thoughts, and begin taking control over them.

Remember the little kid I described in the earlier chapters? I was the shy, dumb, unconfident, burned-out, peed-pants kid. I had a poverty mindset. I couldn't see my future. I never felt like I fitted in. I felt aimless and lacked purpose in my life. That was me, and that mentality carried over well into my forties. I'm now fifty-three years old, at the time of this writing, and I finally understand that my future is only limited by the limits I put on myself. I am so passionate about what has happened to me that I have to share my experience, to help you get what you want and become your greater purpose, too. It's a process of self-discovery, hard lessons, failures and willingness to grow. The process of becoming the person you're aiming for will require time, repetition, introspection, honesty, and many new neural pathways that support your new beliefs.

As you progress through this book, it is important that you take time for introspection, restructuring your thought habits and replacing limiting beliefs with messages that you have unlimited potential. You cannot depend on others to give the affirmations you need. And you don't need others to do it. You can reprogram yourself through constant repetition and reinforcement. Watch videos. Read books. Create new experiences. Do whatever it takes to immerse yourself in the messages and skills you need to grow. This is imperative. You can begin by writing the qualities you intuitively know that you need, to become the person you want to become, and then start internalizing those beliefs through daily reading, repetition and experiences.

This may sound like simple affirmations, but becoming your greater purpose will take much more than repeating wishful thinking. In *The Miracle Morning*, Hal Elrod explains that reciting affirmations is not enough. He says that we need to ground our beliefs in commitment, rather than attempting to trick our subconscious into believing something that is not true. For example, a typical affirmation is: *"I am wealthy and money comes to me easily."* Elrod claims that a more effective affirmation is: *"I am committed to doing what it takes to be wealthy."* This type of affirmation reinforces your belief that you are committed to becoming wealthy, and communicates a truthful directive to your subconscious that you will take an active role in accomplishing the goal. So, if you've tried *The Secret's* version of manifestation, and it didn't work like it was promised, this may help.

Here are a few more examples of affirmations that work. These examples align with a growth mindset and internal locus of control, and support a view of forward progress, with effort and time. Read them. Apply them to your life. Replace your cat video consumption with these thoughts:

I AM COMMITTED:
I am (committed to) constantly developing.
I am (committed to) becoming persistent.
I am (growing increasingly) thoughtful.
I am (committed to) giving more.
I am increasingly becoming healthy, wealthy and wise.
I am committed to becoming a better listener.
I am committed to becoming increasingly capable.
I am increasingly intelligent.
I am committed to becoming a better communicator.
I am increasingly bold.
I am increasingly fearless.
I am increasingly loving and caring.
Whatever... keep going.

While writing those affirmations, I was reminded of the scene in the movie *The Help*, when Aibileen Clark told the little girl: "You is kind. You is smart. You is important." Aibileen reinforced those words, over and over, including the scene when the little girl pottied in her front yard. The child's mother was furious and spanked her, but Aibileen comforted the little girl and whispered: "You is kind. You is smart. You is important." It's a beautiful reminder that self-talk can impact how you see yourself, in spite of the deluge of negativity coming from social media, family, friends and your own thoughts.

I have used affirmations for a few years now. My list has changed over time, and they will change again at some point, but the present list is what I use today. It is what I am becoming. I print this list every time I edit it, and have it in a picture frame on my desk. I read it (or certain parts I really want to focus on) daily. However, it's not enough to simply read these words and expect magic to happen. You need to visualize yourself taking actions that require those traits. You need to then take action, every day, to reinforce those beliefs. Creating new neural connections requires action, experience, repetition and, if you're really enjoying what you're working on, pleasant emotions will speed up the process. As an example, if you want to become a better communicator, you have to tell yourself: "I'm increasingly becoming an excellent communicator, and people listen to me and take me seriously." Then you have to immerse yourself in learning to become a communicator. Read books on the subject. Go to seminars. Watch public speakers and practice speaking. Instead of scrolling through TikTok or Instagram, watching random videos, search for articles on communication in the workplace. Find out when and where your local Toastmasters (speaking club) meets and start attending. And then participate. Don't hesitate, just do it.

You can absolutely become the person required to become your greater purpose, if you reinforce the skills and thoughts needed with action, experiences and repetition. Your mind will begin creating new neural pathways around your ability to communicate well, and soon you'll not only believe that you're a good communicator, you will *become* a good communicator, not only because you visualized it, but because you told yourself (the truth) that you are becoming an excellent communicator, and because you began taking action, over and over, to make it so.

This is possible with nearly any skill, any trait and any passion, as long as you are committed to the process. You'll need patience and grace for yourself. And you'll need a growth mindset and internal locus of control.

I suggest you make a list like the one above, and adjust it as you continue to reflect on the person you are becoming. This will begin the process of propagandizing yourself and building the person you want to become. This is an important step, because you have to get in a healthy place and build a growth mindset before you can become your greater purpose. If you try to find a greater purpose for your life when you're still blinded by your possibilities (fixed mindset), you will be disappointed. If you're still thinking with an external locus of control, one failure and you'll start pointing fingers and finding fault. This process is about fixing your mindset before you begin the ongoing process of brainwashing yourself into becoming someone more capable. It's about starting to believe what's possible. It's about beginning to understand that you are worthy of becoming the person you were meant to become.

Some people call this process "fake it until you make it", and that's what it is. It's what you've done your whole life. Everyone does it. When you were a kid, you wanted to be a teenager; when you were a teenager, you wanted to be an adult; when you became an adult, you took on ever-increasing responsibilities, even if you weren't really qualified yet; you were striving to become someone more capable, until it was true. It's called maturing. It's called living. It's called becoming. This is what school is for. This is what apprenticeships are for. This is what training is all about: to show someone how to improve over time. But, what's great about the process of becoming your greater purpose, when paired with a growth mindset and internal locus of control, is that you can become whatever you want. It's a focused, targeted becoming process. So, let the naysayers be naysayers; you become you.

Here's my daily program. It's fluid, always changing, always improving, and that's the idea. Becoming my greater purpose requires me to become the person capable of accomplishing my goals. The more ambitious my goals become, the more I need to improve. Becoming your greater purpose isn't easy. It's not a passive idea. It's about creating a new you, made of substance and effort, not fluff.

The top line is my **WHY**: my mission. The second line is my **MODE**: how I accomplish my mission.

POSITIVELY HELPING INDIVIDUALS AND TEAMS GET WHAT THEY WANT:

"By purposefully dreaming, responsibly developing, focusing and taking action, I get what I want, reach my full potential and become my greater purpose."

I care. I give. I lead.
Helping others succeed is my greatest ambition.
I am committed to becoming a successful author, speaker and coach.
The right words change lives.

I am constantly developing. Change is good.
I am an instrument of the Creator.
I have unlimited potential.

I help others reach their full potential.

I speak life, love and encouragement to others.
I am committed to bringing high value to teams and individuals.
I am committed to excellence.
I am increasingly healthy, wealthy and wise.

My body is constantly rebuilding my cells to their perfect state.
My heart, liver, lungs, kidneys, bones, muscles and nervous, cardiovascular and immune systems are healthy and strong.
My brain and memory are sharp and acute.

I have an abundance of creative ideas.
The more I give, the more I receive.
I see value in everyone, in every circumstance.
I meet good and trustworthy mentors.
I'm here to bring value, in a unique manner specifically designed by the Creator.
My subconscious mind accepts and makes all of these things so.

"As someone thinks within himself, so he is." Proverbs 23:7.

Spend some time building your list. Begin by asking yourself what you want. Think about the person you have to become to accomplish your dream. Edit your list as you change and grow. This is a trial run; it's just an exercise; it isn't permanent. Have fun with your list and use your imagination. Here are a few questions to help stimulate the process of figuring out <u>what you need</u> to get what you want.

What do I want?

What would it take for that to happen?

What do I need to know, to get what I want?

Who do I need to become, to get what I want?

What do I need to change or correct in me, to get what I want?

What character traits do I need to get what I want?

What skills do I need to get what I want?

How can I gain/qualify for those skills?

How do I sustain the energy to get what I want?

You have been becoming your greater purpose your entire life. You've had ups and downs, and made a lot of mistakes. That's okay, those mistakes have contributed to your life, experiences and knowledge; you can learn from those mistakes and start building the life you want. But you will need a growth mindset, an internal locus of control, and you will need to know what you want. Now, let's begin honing-in on who you are becoming and where you're going.

Your past made a contribution to who you are becoming. It's what makes you passionate about who you want to become, or who you don't want to become. Use that passion, paired with forgiveness, and focus on what's ahead, not what's behind you. Know that all of your stories were stepping-stones to becoming someone better, someone who walked a trail that no one else has traveled. Now start thinking about where that trail will take you.

Chapter review.

- What is your major takeaway from this chapter? How can you apply it to your life today?
- What action steps can you begin taking today, to start making even the smallest changes?
- If you haven't already done it, write your *"I Am Committed"* list. This list will begin steering you toward becoming the person capable of getting what you want and reaching your full potential.
- Evaluate your mindset and begin developing Carol Dweck's *"5 Beliefs of a Growth Mindset"* into your daily life. Write them, read them, apply them every day.
- Evaluate your locus of control. Begin by evaluating whether you're more "external" or "internal". Develop an external locus of control by writing, reading and applying the following: *"I have control over my life, choices and results. I do not give that power to anyone."*
- Is there someone you trust, with whom you can work through this book as an accountability partner? If so, call them today.

Chapter 6

HOW EVERYTHING CHANGED

"Success is peace of mind which is a direct result of self-satisfaction in knowing you did your best to become the best you are capable of becoming."

John Wooden

In 2003, I completed my four-year apprenticeship and earned journeyman status as a card-carrying pipefitter. I was thirty-three years old and married, with four children. Those were wonderful years, raising our babies, building a life, continuing my college education, learning a trade and growing spiritually. It's not as if my life was gloomy – it wasn't – but you have to understand that what was working on the outside did not reflect what I felt on the inside, because old neural habits are hard to break.

Most men, from what I understood, weighed their personal worth based on their family, spiritual community, work and their contribution to society. I was no different, although, outside of my family and spiritual life, nothing seemed to be working. There was no answer. Work was just work, I thought; end of story. I guess I thought I'd find meaning with a college degree, but I didn't. I thought I'd get it with a journeyman's card; I didn't. I thought I'd find it when I started my own business – nope, not there, either. The doubts and insecurities that formed in my youth were still haunting me, still telling me, "I'm stupid," and, "I'm less," and, "I'm not going anywhere."

Without understanding why I felt this way, it seemed that this record in my head would play indefinitely. And, to be honest, I felt the same with my kids, too. My wife spent more time with them, and she is much better at nurturing. I felt like she had a bond with them that I would never have. I tried passing on knowledge and good values, and assuring them that they were loved, no matter what. But there were many times when I wondered if I was a good dad. I wondered if they were going to turn out okay, and I felt like it would be my fault if they didn't, because I was working so much, or a plethora of other unsubstantiated reasons.

Even as a grown-ass man, I was still stuck in my early programming. I didn't know it, but I had given control of my life to the lies that were wired into my neural pathways. I didn't have control over my mindset. It didn't matter if I failed or succeeded; I still believed that I was dumb, adrift and less.

Soon after I earned journeyman status as a pipefitter, I quit my job at Chrysler and started a home-maintenance business. At the time, I was working in a skilled trades position which, in my community, was considered one of the pre-eminent blue-collar jobs. With overtime, it was easily a six-figure income. Why would I quit that? What could possibly be missing? That's a good question, and I think that's what I was ultimately searching for: the thing that was missing.

Over the course of my adult life, I had worked as an HVAC installer, laborer, assembly worker, pipefitter and, in 2003, ventured into self-employment. On the outside, Jeff Bennington could do anything – or so it would appear. But Jeff was actually trying to find significance, and he was failing fast. Four years into running my business into the ground, I went back to the factory. In late 2006, I took a position as a pipefitter at the local General Motors plant. And that's when things started to change for me.

In 2007, after realizing that I was right back where I was a few years prior, and feeling bored in a job that only required a few hours of work in a twelve-hour shift, I thought about writing. I thought about writing because I remembered how much I enjoyed "blue book" exams when I was in college, and I remembered how much I enjoyed writing my own Sunday school curriculum when that was a part of my life. I didn't know what I'd write about – I felt like my life was pretty dull, pretty normal – but I needed to fill my time and direct my creative energy somewhere, and the right-brain, daydreaming side of me was itching to get out. So, I used my downtime and wrote a little book called *How to Be Successful in the Handyman Business.* Sounds like a noteworthy accomplishment? Well, let me tell you, I ended up throwing my only printed version into the fire, and then deleted the file on my computer, because that book caused a lot of pain. After working on the book for a few months, I gleefully presented it to my wife. When she started reading, I could see the pain all over her face.

"You call those four years a success? The business consumed you. We were living on credit card debt. And you practically missed the first couple of years of your daughter's life."

Failure.

Worthless.

Stupid.

Less.

I agreed.

I immediately kindled a fire in our fireplace and threw the manuscript into the flames. I then deleted the file on our MacBook, right in front of her. I never rewrote it.

I went back to work, and things were stable for a while, because I realized that she was right. I wasn't being honest with myself. I had written a book filled with half-truths, sharing the things I had done right but not what I had done wrong. I realized something else, though: I discovered that I loved writing. The process of putting my thoughts and imaginings on paper felt freeing. It was as if there was a part of me that was trying to bloom for my entire life – the creative and daydreamy side – but it would get snuffed out by teachers, by parents, by my wife.

That, of course, was my perception, based on my insecurities and distorted view of the world; my faulty mindset. In retrospect, no one was maliciously attempting to harm me; that's just how I processed conflict. Yet, despite that failure, something exciting was happening. For the third time in my life, I discovered a piece of me that needed to be investigated: first, drumming; second, running; third, writing. I was becoming someone; I just didn't know who that was yet.

I enjoyed writing, so I did more of that. By 2009, I had penned my first novel, *Killing the Giants*, an action-packed conspiracy theory made for the big screen. The book was amazing. I had no doubt that readers would line up at bookstores across the globe, to shake my hand and pay top dollar for a signed copy. Secretively, I dreamed that Denzel Washington would come knocking on my door, begging to take the lead role.

Okay, you can stop laughing now. I told you I have a wild imagination. Unfortunately, like many first-time authors, my excitement quickly waned once the reviews started coming in and sales dropped off a cliff, after pushing the book on my friends and family.

"Poor writing skills," one reviewer stated.

"Littered with adjectives," said another.

I felt humiliated. I had so many questions. After sharing my discouragement with my wife, I asked: "What's an adjective?"

Clearly, I had much to learn.

While drowning in self-pity, I remembered the skills I had learned as a paperboy, grass cutter, factory worker, HVAC installer and pipefitter: I was a hard worker and persistent. If there was anything I could do right, it was working hard. And, for the first time in my life, I actually took an honest look at myself and asked what I could do to get better. Rather than make an excuse for my failure, or blame others for stifling my creativity, I asked what it would take to *not* have poor writing skills; how could I improve? I didn't blame my teachers. I didn't blame my parents. I took one hundred percent responsibility for my failure, and that was a big deal, because this seemingly logical step would later become an essential part of my transformational experience.

I immediately started reading books on writing and all forms of literature. This was my first attempt at personal development. At the age of thirty-nine, I had finally made a choice to dig into a topic that I was passionate about, because it had become abundantly clear that I didn't know what I was doing. Sure, I was creative, and there were signs that I had what it took to become a writer - I was capable of transferring my vision into fiction, and I had enough ideas to throw 80,000 or more words down on paper – but I knew very little about character development, plot structure or other techniques that enriched the reading experience. So, I began a process that would eventually change my life.

The truth was, I wasn't a good writer, but I wanted to become one. Therefore, I committed to reading a book of fiction and a book on writing, and then, afterward, writing a short story, to practice what I had learned. I did this until I felt like I was ready for another novel. After writing the next novel, I would do it again, and then again, and then again, and then again. I did this for seven years.

You can see these steps below. The process is much like the example I demonstrated in the previous chapter, on becoming an excellent communicator. This process demonstrates exactly how getting what you want requires thought, vision, action and repetition. It's a process I call deep immersion.

Here's the immersive process I went through to become a writer, after failing miserably:

WRITE BOOK 1: *Killing the Giants*

Read: *Ernest Hemingway on Writing*, by Larry W. Phillips.

Read: *Dracula*, by Bram Stoker.

WRITE A SHORT STORY: *The Rumblin'*

Read: *Novelist's Boot Camp*, by Todd A. Stone.

Read: *Moby Dick*, by Herman Melville.

WRITE BOOK 2: *Reunion*

Read: *Write like the Masters*, by William Cane.

Read: *IT*, by Stephen King.

WRITE A SHORT STORY: *Murdoch's Eyes*

Read: *On Writing*, by Stephen King.

Read: *The Grapes of Wrath*, by John Steinbeck.

WRITE BOOK 3: *Creepy* **(a 3-book series)**

Read: *Watchers*, by Dean Koontz.

Read: *Writing the Breakout Novel*, by Donald Maass.

WRITE BOOK 4: *The Secret in Defiance* (with Patrick Bousum)

AND SO ON...

At this point, my blog, *The Writing Bomb*, was taking off, so I aggregated many of my blog posts, on the lessons I was learning about writing and self-publishing, into a book for authors: *The Indie Author's Guide to the Universe*. This book was later retitled: *The Indie Author's Guide to Publishing Success*. During this period, my blog was growing so fast that I had to create a WordPress website which could handle the traffic and give me more flexibility. In the process, we renamed our site *The Kindle Book Review*, and within a few years it was one of the top websites for independent authors. We monetized it and soon had over 47,000 subscribers, made up of authors and readers. Today, it is an award-winning website and, at the time of this writing, is in the twelfth season of its International English-Speaking Literary Awards.

When we started The Kindle Book Awards, we had no idea how successful it would become, and I had no idea how many books I would enjoy. We had dozens of volunteers who would read and review the many submissions that came in every day. Our top book reviewers, including myself, would read through hundreds of book submissions. I usually took the Horror/Suspense category, because that was my favorite fiction genre. Over the next several years, I would read dozens of award-winning, self-published books, connect with hundreds of authors and dozens of service providers in the industry, and at times get paid to consult, edit, design book covers, develop new ideas for the website and co-write books with other authors, all while working my day job as a pipefitter, repairing leaking pipes and working around toxic chemicals.

Over time, this dumb, nervous, shy, peed-pants, insecure kid who, only a few years earlier, had felt aimless in his career, small among his peers, purposeless and stuck in a job where I was fixing clogged toilets, was moving in a completely different direction. I was changing rapidly, learning lessons that would change my life forever. I was becoming a writer, and learning that many of the messages I had come to believe about myself were not true. I had come to understand that I was taught many things about life, money and people that were completely wrong.

I was immersed in reading, writing, editing and working with other writers, and the constant repetition was building a new person. After writing hundreds of thousands of words, I was becoming an author. I was becoming a content creator. I was becoming a book cover designer. New neural habits and skills were forming, and I was becoming more than I thought was ever possible.

Obviously, my inability to sit still was not the problem my teachers claimed it was; it was one of my greatest strengths, because I had the energy to work twelve or more hours a day, doing something I loved, and it never felt like work. My energy and enthusiasm were attractive to my coworkers and fellow authors. The old program was showing cracks in the system. I don't blame my teachers or parents for driving those messages into me; they didn't understand the value in those quirks. No one did back then.

My daydreaming used to be a problem, but it, too, was actually one of my greatest strengths. My ability to organize a creative idea, into an engaging novel or short story that would impact readers, gave me an incredible sense of accomplishment and purpose. That same creativity became useful on the website, too, because I was constantly coming up with new and interesting ways to market books, and find solutions to an array of problems that have contributed to other successes in my life.

Another issue I had was fear: fear of everything. Fear that I'd say something stupid among the giants in my life. Fear of failure. Fear of not being loved. Fear of getting mugged or beaten up. My fear list could go on and on. However, my many fears were also one of my greatest strengths. I used those fears to build my characters, because we all have fears. No one understood that more than I did. Therefore, I now better understand many of my fears by living vicariously through my characters. I don't know if this is an author thing or not, but it was definitely true for me.

This period of my life taught me many lessons, and began to form a foundation of understanding what it really means to be successful. I was learning what it meant to succeed in a temporal sense, and what it takes to accomplish any goal. I was learning that there were common traits among the successful people I was meeting. And I met a lot of successful authors online, and a variety of people I would have never met without *The Kindle Book Review.*

I learned a lot from writing, and from the many years of aimlessly chasing. I learned how to persist through challenges. I learned the value of personal development and accepting criticism. I learned how to envision and construct a big idea, and polish the details. The art of taking an idea and building it out to completion, editing, formatting and publishing took many skills; what I discovered was that those skills could be applied to almost any objective.

After all that writing, I had put on about thirty pounds, because I was sitting way too much and not eating very well. After seeing myself in a family photo, I decided I needed to make some changes, so I adjusted my diet and started running again. It had been years since I had run, so I was really out of shape. Before long, I made a Facebook promise stating that I was going to run a marathon, a goal that had been on my bucket list for a long time. Six months and a few shin splints later, I completed my first 26.2-mile race. And that's when I made my next goal: to qualify for the Boston Marathon. This was an important goal, because I never went to "state" in cross country, though I came really close – and that always felt like another failure to me. My senior year in high school, our team made it to semi-state, and I ran my best race ever. However, only the top ten individual finishers went to the state finals. After the first half mile, no one else passed me. I passed hundreds of runners – unfortunately, I didn't pass enough of them. There was a pack of five runners in front of me who I didn't have time to catch, and I missed going to the state finals by a few seconds.

With that said, I needed to qualify for the Boston Marathon, to prove to myself that I was a capable runner. I needed to know that I could accomplish it, because it was possible and because I wanted to. I needed to know if I could set a bucket-list goal and accomplish it, like I did with my books. The burning question for me was: *Am I a one-hit wonder, or can someone actually make a realistic goal and accomplish it, no matter how difficult it is? Were my previous successes a fluke?*

Long story short, after four attempts, and several injuries later, I qualified for the Boston Marathon, at the Indianapolis Monumental Marathon in November 2016, with a time of 3:22.20. I was forty-six years old. Although that goal was interrupted by injuries, doubts about my capabilities and lessons about what it took to run a marathon, I did it.

Accomplishing that goal took my mindset to another level. Not only had I learned that my childhood programming about myself, others and the world around me was often wrong, I had proven to myself that I can achieve anything, with perseverance and a willingness to learn. This opened an entirely new world to me, and taught me a slew of other critical lessons about becoming, that I want to share with you, because you have aspirations and dreams of your own, and I want you to get what you want. Let me be very clear, I do not believe success is all about money; success is just an idea, it's not about money. Money can come as a result of success, but true success is when you realize that you're capable of more than you thought possible, and then apply those capabilities in a way that delivers value and meaning to you and others.

What I learned was how important it was for me to stop relying on myself and rely on others – for coaching, input and feedback. And this was just one habit that was keeping me from growing. I always thought that I would have gone to state if my coach had done something different, never accepting personal responsibility, but the lesson I learned from writing was that I must change. I must take responsibility and be open to learning something I didn't know, and that I could be wrong about anything. I mean, when you write a book, and the world according to Amazon says that you're not a good writer, you're forced to accept the truth. There are many times when I could have taken greater responsibility. Ultimately, there is no one else to blame, nor should I look for that.

I grew up around a fixed mindset, where there was an abundance of criticism. Rarely did I hear, "I'm sorry, it's my fault," or, "Keep trying," or, "You've got this." That's the language of a growth mindset; it's encouraging and inspirational. Thinking of myself as "becoming" was transformational. If I'm not fixed and my future isn't fixed, I began asking, what could I become?

Suddenly, becoming was an option I'd never heard of. In my mind, I had limited potential, limited brainpower and limited possibilities. But, when I started listening to Jim Rohn and others speaking the growth language, I'd hear phrases like: "Becoming more valuable. Becoming more skilled. Becoming wiser. Becoming better, stronger, smarter." I finally got it. The idea that I can become better began to sink in. The idea that I can become someone more valuable inspired me.

Jim Rohn was yet another mentor to me, although I never met him. His words were spoken with a stern love that impacted my belief in myself. Jim said: "If you want to have more, you have to become more. For things to change, *you* have to change. For things to get better, *you* have to become better. If you improve, everything will improve for you. If you grow, your money will grow. Your relationships, your health, your business and every external effect will mirror that growth, in equal correlation."

Wow! I had never heard anything like that before. I had heard the term personal development, but I always thought that was for the Tony Robbins-, new-age types, who'd get all excited over the weekend, but slip right back into their old habits as soon as the bliss wore off. I had no idea that real change was possible, especially for me. The idea of taking responsibility for what I wanted, and setting goals to get there, and believing I was capable of more, really started to sink in.

This is where things get juicy. While attempting to qualify for the Boston Marathon, I was simultaneously working on another writing project with the same objective: to reach a goal on demand. Was it possible? Could I do this again?

Obviously, there can be physical and time limitations to our desires. I'm 5'5" tall and 150 pounds; therefore, I will never become a professional football player. However, if I want to become a doctor, or a lawyer, or an architect, I can. And so can you! But I wasn't interested in those disciplines; I wanted to become a published author – a real author, certified by a legitimate publisher. A real author is paid an advance for the rights to a book, for a designated period of time, and there is an agreement between the publisher and author that the publisher will edit, produce and distribute the book in exchange for an agreed percentage of the sales. In my eyes, this was the real deal. Until that time, I thought of myself as only a self-published author. The idea of getting published would validate that my hard work had turned into skill. Becoming a published author was my next objective, and I believed that I had a formula to accomplish that goal. If the formula worked, I knew that anything was possible for this insecure, peed-pants punk.

After months of hard work, my tenth book, *Federal Underground*, was published by an Amazon imprint in September 2016. I accepted the contract and was paid the coveted advance. Two years later, we sold *The Kindle Book Review* and I made a career change, taking a sales position with a global HVAC manufacturer. I inherited a downtrodden territory and I had no sales experience, but I used the same formula for success, and turned a $3.5 million territory into a $7 million territory in two years, being awarded a top-ten national sales award. My new mindset and the lessons I'd learned were working, but there was still something missing.

At this point in my life, I didn't have a personal mission statement or vision for my life. I didn't know my greater purpose. I had heard the terms in passing, but thought they were fluffy and irrelevant words – but I was wrong. I was missing some of the major keys to success and becoming. I had learned many of the traits that were creating success in my life, like taking full responsibility, getting laser-focused and taking massive action. But there were more important lessons to be learned.

To be clear, becoming your greater purpose doesn't mean that you have to be perfect; that will never happen. If you're looking for a greater purpose in your life, you must always keep your eyes open for ways to grow, improve and remain humble. Having a greater purpose involves becoming and developing into what could be, not looking back on what could have been. When you're becoming your greater purpose, you'll discover that you're taking on many of the traits of highly successful people: persistent, grateful, learns from others, a good listener, a reader, willing to take risks, a team player, a servant, encouraging, good character, an influencer, among other traits. This is why it is so important to reconstruct your mindset and beliefs about yourself first. As these characteristics become part of you, you'll begin wondering where you fit into the grand scheme of life. You'll start asking questions about how you can make a difference in the lives of others, who you're equipped to serve, and other questions related to your significance. You'll begin to see problems that you are uniquely qualified to solve, and how you can grow into a more capable person, to tackle even bigger things. This is when success shifts into becoming.

> *"Knowing others is intelligence. Knowing yourself is true wisdom. Mastering others is strength. Mastering yourself is true power."*
>
> Lao Tzu

As you traverse through life, there isn't a line in the sand, where you're either successful on one side or a failure on the other. Life doesn't work like that. You become your greater purpose by the richness of your life, and over time you navigate through a unique set of circumstances, people, occupations and lessons that only you will experience. The ups and downs in living are meant to transform you into a stronger, more resilient and capable person. It's a process and it's messy. Life is messy. And becoming your greater purpose demands that you slip, fall and make a mess every once in a while, because without your unique failures and mistakes, what value can you bring to the world, that the world hasn't already experienced itself? Without a little carnage of your own, how can you have empathy for anyone else?

The process of becoming your greater purpose will require you to be open and grateful for your life, as it is right now. It will require you to learn to love your life now, to love yourself now, and to find purpose and meaning in your life now, whatever state you are in. You can always find something to be grateful for. The capacity to find the smallest grain of purpose and meaning right now is yet another muscle that, when exercised, will stretch, grow and expand your ability to find purpose going forward. This is why I spent so much time sharing my story and encouraging you to examine yours. You are becoming, and, if you are brave enough, you will continue to become your greater purpose every day for the rest of your life. If you think you have "found" your greater purpose, and you stop there, you are no longer growing, expanding or learning. Becoming never stops. Becoming is always a new beginning, through every season of your life. It's a process. It's a mindset.

The process of becoming your greater purpose, however, requires that you apply a few rules, as you develop into a more capable version of yourself. Yes, you will need to hit certain growth milestones to live the life of purpose and meaning you're after. Cutting corners, like any good work, will result in poor quality, and this is true for anything, including finding meaning in your life and becoming a quality person. Think about it: how can you become your greater purpose if you can't become a greater you? Deepak Chopra said: "If you focus on success, you'll have stress. But if you pursue excellence, success will be guaranteed." And that's why much of the rest of this book is focusing on building a better you, and teaching you what excellent people do to succeed.

Becoming is the essence of the growth mindset. Becoming. Growing. Developing. They all mean the same thing. If you think of yourself as becoming, you will become whatever you wish. Becoming is a trait that can become part of your identity, just like, "I'm curious," or, "I'm eager," or, "I'm a hard worker." I'm becoming. Becoming is fast-forwarding evolution; we either become better or we go backward.

French novelist Anais Nin said: *"Life is a process of becoming, a combination of states we have to go through. Where people fail is that they wish to elect a state and remain in it. This is a kind of death."*

Staying where you are is comfortable now. Staying where you are, however, is a vote in favor of regret. Tony Robbins said: "Life is a gift, and it offers us the privilege, opportunity and responsibility to give something back, by becoming more."

I've learned a lot about growing and developing, because of my many experiences. My interest in personal development has taught me how highly successful people accomplish their goals, and the laws that guide them. Even those who care nothing about money, who live their greater purpose, still follow these rules. Therefore, having a truly meaningful purpose will require you to develop yourself, by following "The Six Laws of Becoming". This is how becoming a greater purpose works. The six laws are incorporated in the following sentence:

"By purposefully dreaming, responsibly developing, focusing and taking action, you accomplish your goals and become

your greater purpose."

That sentence summarizes the mechanics of becoming your greater purpose. When you approach "The Six Laws of Becoming" with a winning mindset, you are ready to reach your full potential. There are six components; all are required. But there's one more ingredient to the laws that you won't see; it's invisible. It's your character. It's your faith. It's your understanding that a person with poor character can follow all of these rules to the tee, and still fail at finding meaning. Your character is the glue that binds all of these laws together. Living a life with purpose requires doing what's right when no one is looking. Living a life of purpose requires empathy. Living a life of purpose requires you to be upstanding, be truthful and care about people and the world around you. And, in my experience, this is not always intuitive. When left to ourselves, we become self-absorbed. When we seek a higher power, we are more likely to take our eyes off ourselves. Helping and caring for others is a significant part of any spiritual journey.

If you're already in that place, you're ready for the next steps. If you're not, I urge you to take a deeper look inside and consider where your values come from. Don't miss the spiritual connection in the process of your becoming. It's important. It's the secret ingredient, custom-designed to complete the masterpiece that you are becoming. I don't know what rabbit-hole that will take you down, but becoming a person of character, with hope and love, is a path that is extremely personal and critical to your journey. So, find your spiritual glue, because it will hold "The Six Laws of Becoming" together.

THE SIX LAWS OF BECOMING:

1. Responsibility.

2. Vision.

3. *Focus.*

4. *Purpose.*

5. *Development.*

6. *Action.*

Without these six components, the idea of a greater purpose will remain just that: an idea, a wish, a dream, a fluffy concept lacking any true substance. If you think you can live your greater purpose without these, then there's a pretty good chance that, five years from now, you'll still be searching for a meaningful existence. Like gravity and thermodynamics, there are universal laws that govern success of every kind, including successfully living a good life, successfully becoming the best version of yourself and successfully becoming your greater purpose.

In the remaining chapters, we'll dig into these six laws, to discover how they fit into becoming your greater purpose, and why they're so critical to the process of finding meaning and direction in your life.

Part 2

THE SIX LAWS OF BECOMING

"To reach your potential, you must grow. And, to grow, you must be highly intentional about it."

John C. Maxwell

Chapter 7

RESPONSIBILITY

"The instant you accept responsibility for everything in your life is the moment you acquire the power to change it."

Ed Mylett

Becoming your greater purpose is a lifelong journey. Becoming your greater purpose is not a one-and-done activity, where you write your favorite things to do and pick the activity that sounds the most fun. Becoming your greater purpose is about looking at the entirety of your life and examining how you're wired, building a winning mindset, and figuring out what you want from life and then successfully plotting your course, with a clear vision, purpose and action plan, while remaining flexible when unexpected events hit the brakes on your goals. It's about carefully considering your personality and your passions, and developing yourself into the person required to accomplish your dream. Successfully living a greater purpose takes so much more than thinking good thoughts, and visualizing what you want.

The bigger your vision, the more development required on your part. You can have whatever you want out of life but, depending on where you're starting from, your expectations of the effort required must be aligned with your expected results. Bigger dreams require a bigger effort; an average effort will yield an average result. In other words, you reap what you sow. This isn't a new idea. What's new is that science proves you can create the tools (a winning mindset), to create better soil for your dreams to take root. "The Six Laws of Becoming" will teach you how to become whatever you want, but the first law is the foundation.

At this point, it's clear that I traveled down many different paths. Some of those experiences felt unfulfilling. Sure, sometimes I felt like I was in the wrong place, but I met some incredible people, mastered a few skills and learned a lot about myself. I learned that, when I felt like a square peg in a round hole, I needed to remain committed, as long as I was taking a paycheck. I learned to get the job done, even though it may not be fulfilling or my "dream job". I learned to do the work to the best of my ability, because I owed it to my employer, and because I needed to take care of my family. I also learned that, if I can gain a new skill, even if I'm not super-passionate about it, it may come in handy later. It's important to understand this, because feeling lost and aimless is not really a problem in the scope of discovering your greater purpose; it's the process you must go through to become your greater purpose. It's also possible that, when you feel restless, you might be growing your character, by learning what it means to be loyal and what it takes to persevere. Learning is the key. Learning what doesn't work isn't a problem, it's just another step forward on your path to becoming.

I learned that becoming your greater purpose is about releasing fear, resentment and the people who have hurt you. Becoming your greater purpose requires you to be agnostic about taking risks and change. To do this, you make a plan for your life, plot the course to get there and start moving. This requires a certain level of agnosticism. You must be agnostic because, after weighing the risks and still desiring to go forward with a big dream, you have to dive in, without the biases from your past and fears of the future getting in the way. And, when things don't work out the way you thought, you need to keep your emotions in check and be willing to start over, learning from your mistakes. When you're agnostic about your plans, you remove the self-sabotaging head trash and simply charge forward. This is how people get things done. Electricians don't worry about the risks; they consider them, take the necessary safety measures and get to work. Millwrights don't worry about the hazards of falling several stories; they consider the danger, take proper precautions and start climbing. Everyone feels overwhelmed when standing at the foot of a mountain. You look up and it seems impossible to climb but, once you've made a plan, you put your head down and take one step at a time. On occasion, you look up and make sure you're headed in the right direction. You look back at the trail you've laid out and take another step, and then another, and then another. Pretty soon you'll feel really proud of how far you've come. High-five yourself, or someone on your team, and keep moving forward!

Sounds easy, right? But there were several more lessons I had to learn, that I wish someone had told me when I was young. Unless someone tells you that successful people follow these laws, you inevitably have to figure them out for yourself. You either learn from heartache, monetary losses or time lost.

I never heard about "The Six Laws of Becoming" when I was growing up. I never received a list from my teachers or professors. Oh, sure, I'd hear bits and pieces here and there, but parents and other mentors never came right out and said: "Look, kid, this is exactly what it takes for you to succeed at anything. Just follow the plan. One, two, three, four, five, six – easy." You would think the six laws are common sense, but they're not, unless they're modeled and talked about when you're young. And, even if they were, youngsters can have a tendency to resist boring talk about life lessons that apply far into the future.

However, "The Six Laws of Becoming" are available in literature, millionaire success stories, history books, conferences, mentoring and speeches throughout history. But you have to look for them as if searching for buried treasure; seek and you will find. And there lies the challenge: seeking and removing the roadblocks that are keeping you from getting what you want. Becoming your greater purpose is like removing large stones from a cave: for every stone you clear away, another falls back in its place, and yet you keep working until you clear the path. This can feel frustrating at times, but take heart: you have a growth mindset and you're just not there yet. "The Six Laws of Becoming" will help you dig out of your cave and back into the light.

You can't reach your full potential without applying "The Six Laws of Becoming". Without them, your greater purpose won't feel so great; it will only feel imaginary, a dream tucked away in your wish-list, waiting for someday to land in your lap. And this is really important to understand: if a greater purpose is what you're looking for, you will need each component, because they are dependent upon each other. For example, you need a powerful reason for your vision, so that you can build your dream with focused goals, helpful habits and a personal development plan to make it possible. They all work together and contribute to the process of becoming the person required to reach your full potential.

In this chapter, we're going to focus on the first "law of becoming":

Law #1: RESPONSIBILITY
You must take one hundred percent responsibility to become the person capable of accomplishing your dreams.

No more excuses. No more blaming. No looking back. If you want to become your greater purpose, you have to take full responsibility from this point forward, no matter what your past looks like. This does not mean that you are responsible for any damage you incurred when you were a child; it simply means that you must take responsibility for your life, choices and results from this day forward. You must take one hundred percent responsibility to become the person required to accomplish your goals, and to become your greater purpose. You will need others along the way, and you will need help, but you have to take full responsibility to navigate your journey. No one owes you anything. Every human has his or her own mountains to climb. It's time for you to ascend yours.

I believe you can find meaning and joy in everything when you're intentionally looking for it. I believe you can find peace in knowing that you were thoughtfully created for a time such as this. Without purpose, you're only here by chance, by luck, by accident, and there is no hope in that. However, the overriding morality of humanity seems to suggest that there is a universal code that we're here for the greater good, not individual gratification – so ask yourself, where did that code come from?

I believe we were all meant to serve the world, in some fashion. That's it. Expect anything more from this life and you will be disappointed. You see, when we need others to fulfill our needs, we put the weight of the world on their shoulders. If you cannot embrace that God/The Source/Universal love (whatever you want to call it), loves you and wants the very best for you, you will find yourself demanding your needs from others, and that's not fair to them. Humans were created to help each other, not fill the void in each other's souls. I believe that we are here to help others reach their full potential, not be the source of their potential; that's God's role. You're not God, and neither is anyone else.

You are becoming your greater purpose, and you can help others do the same. Give love, don't demand it. In fact, don't expect it. We can't expect other people, who are just as broken or have the capacity to fail, to fulfill our love needs. If you get that kind of love, rejoice and celebrate it! But others don't owe you love. Focus on improving yourself. Love yourself enough to make the world a better place. Find fulfillment in your faith and your greater purpose, and let others join you.

If you're constantly in need of being in a relationship, or clinging to someone, you're demanding love. If you think you're seeking it, what you're actually doing is expecting the next person to fulfill your love needs and your greater purpose needs. Is it too much to ask for someone to love you? No, absolutely not! But, until you're confident in your own skin and good with the person you're becoming, that neediness will act as a repellent. When you need another person to fill the void, it's not fair to that person. No one is equipped to fill a void that deep; they can never give enough. When they recognize that weight of your demands, they'll either walk away or go into hiding, leaving you right back where you started.

Give more. Take less. Love more. Serve more.

Having said that, it's not selfish to adequately equip yourself to serve your greater purpose. It's not selfish to spend a fraction of each day developing and growing. It's not selfish to be passionate about something that matters, if it serves the greater good. That is far from selfish. That is love. Develop, grow and serve others, without expecting reciprocation – that is what love looks like.

The years I spent writing over half a million words developed a skill and passion in me that I never imagined was possible. That certain something inside of me that was missing had begun to come into view, like a ship far off the coast, breaking through the mist as its form finally appeared. I was a dad. I was a husband. I was a writer. I was creative. I was a problem solver. I was a skilled tradesman. I was a marathoner and a drummer. I was becoming. I could finally see what was happening to me. My life wasn't a series of internal struggles; I was in the process of becoming. The process of discovering *what I'm made of* and *what I'm made for.*

For over forty years, I believed I had limited potential, but that was not true; this had become apparent, at last. Is it possible that kids like me, who spend so many years painfully dredging through life, have unlimited potential? You may hear those words on occasion but, until you change the way you think and change your programming, the idea of being "limitless" may not gel with how you feel about yourself. But, now you know, reaching your full potential is possible. One hundred percent.

Looking back, I can see that my work ethic developed persistence, and my persistence developed grit, and grit developed a skill, and then my skill, paired with a single spark – a single success – created a small sense of accomplishment. That small sense of accomplishment built self-confidence. And it was those small, unseen moments of growth that were building the person I was meant to become. Could this have happened sooner, if I had gone through mindset training as a teen, or as a young adult? Absolutely!

Ed Mylett, businessman, author, speaker and YouTube personality, put it this way: *"Self-confidence is really someone who keeps promises to themselves. Because self-confidence is really your reputation with yourself. If you've got a great reputation with yourself, and you know you can trust you, you're not so concerned about your reputation with what other people think about you."*[11]

Ed's statement resonates with me because, for the longest time, I did not have a great reputation with myself. My little wins here and there were not enough to gain the self-confidence I needed to build a strong internal trust; that would take many successes and years of replacing old thought habits and beliefs, through repetition. And that takes time; for some, this could take months, for others years. Our unique and complex stories dictate the time and energy required to change.

That sounds like a long process and it is. It's a process that has to be repeated, over and over and over again, before thousands of small successes can actually repair (or rewrite) the false beliefs you may have about yourself. And this is what it takes for anyone to change a personal narrative. Anyone who feels the way I did – lost, aimless, without purpose, stupid, small, fearful and unconfident – will have to live through many challenges, in order to build a backlog of experiences that will, in time, serve as your teacher, and as proof that you are not who your past (and your self-talk) says you are. In retrospect, I have learned that life is nothing more than a series of lessons. And the level of meaning and joy you take away from those lessons is determined by how you view those experiences. Do you get better? Or do you get bitter?

Can you drum up the strength to look at the past, kiss it on the forehead, and start over? Are you willing to learn? Are you willing to find out what you're missing? Are you willing to look for the skill and knowledge and character gaps in your life, and take full responsibility to change? If you forgive and then look forward, you'll figure out what do you need to know.

Throughout my life, I've met many people who object to reading: "I'm not a reader," they say. I can't tell you how many times I've heard that. But I totally understand. Reading can seem boring, make you sleepy and you may find it hard to focus. I get it. Sometimes I read the same paragraph, over and over, just to comprehend the content. However, reading isn't any different than working out. When you're out of shape, it's super hard to get started, and it may take a few go-arounds before you get your reading muscles into shape. Think of your focus and comprehension as muscles that need to be conditioned, in small increments, until they are capable of reading more. Start slow. Read just fifteen minutes a day, or every other day, until you get into shape. Or, listen to audiobooks and educational videos, or TED talks, until the hunger for growth gets you excited for more.

Look, if you aren't getting what you want from life, and you don't want to learn from successful people who have written books, telling you how they did it, saving you a lifetime of mistakes and setbacks for the small investment of a paperback, e-book or audiobook, you can expect to repeat the same mistakes they made. Moreover, with today's technology, everything you need to know is available at your fingertips, if you are willing to seek it. There is no excuse for not learning what it takes to accomplish your goals and becoming the person capable of doing it. Heck, there are probably thousands of free (or almost free) audiobooks on YouTube that can get you started. And there's this little-known public storehouse of knowledge that we call a library, where knowledge about practically everything is free.

Like Jim Rohn said: "For things to change, you have to change. When you change, everything changes for you." This statement is absolutely true, because no one has ever turned their life around without changing something in themselves first. Change is one of the master keys to becoming your greater purpose, including changing your learning habits. And there are other laws that we'll get to. But you must understand that, if you have been blaming others for your problems or failures, it's critical for you to start changing yourself, and stop focusing on the need for others to change. You must agree to work on changing yourself as your greatest priority because, when you change, everything will change. This starts by changing what you think about, and there is no easier way to do that than by immersing yourself in books, or other materials that inspire and guide you toward the things you want.

Jim Rohn inspired millions of people around the world. His story epitomizes what it means to become your greater purpose. As a young man, Jim was struggling with the results of his life, and his sense of failure came to a head when he told a lie to a little girl scout who was trying to sell him some cookies. The lie was that he didn't need to buy any cookies, because he said he had plenty of them inside; in truth, he didn't have any money. That bothered him so much that he finally reached out for help. When his mentor asked him about his lack of money, Jim blamed his employer. He blamed the government. He blamed everyone but himself. After his mentor gave him some sage advice, he began working on himself and his entire life turned around. And he has influenced me, too; I now take one hundred percent responsibility for who I am and who I am becoming.

Blaming others for our failures isn't uncommon; many people do this. Only a few intuitively look within themselves to solve their own problems. However, blaming others leaves your development at the mercy of others. Robert Anthony, Harvard professor and public figure, said: "When you blame others, you give up your power to change." J.K. Rowling, author of the *Harry Potter* series, said: "There is an expiry date on blaming your parents for steering you in the wrong direction; the moment you are old enough to take the wheel, responsibility lies with you."

John C. Maxwell, *New York Times* bestselling author and global speaker, wrote: *"People who blame others for their failures never overcome them. They simply move from problem to problem. To reach your potential, you must continually improve yourself, and you can't do that if you don't take responsibility for your actions and learn from your mistakes."*

Learning this lesson changed my life. It was easy to blame my dad for my lack of direction. It was easy to blame my mother for my insecurities. But where did that get me? Nowhere. As a parent, I learned that you don't always know what you're doing; you're winging it most of the time, doing the best you can to deal with the crazy, unpredictable things kids do. Today, there are endless resources for parenting and relationships, but information wasn't as readily available for my parents; their only resource was the example their parents set for them. By learning to take responsibility for my results, over the course of my life, I've learned that if I take one hundred percent responsibility for my choices and results, I am free to move forward. And I have. Don't miss the end; you'll want to know how my relationships with my parents turned out.

When you blame others for your failures, it's like staying in a dark cave, knowing there's a mountain outside with a breathtaking view, but choosing to stay in the shadows because you're vitriolic and pouting. You feel safe, but it's a path to nowhere. Removing the blame game from your modus operandi is like walking out of the cave and climbing to the crest, where you can see for miles. The view is spectacular. From there, you can go anywhere you want. You can see possibilities and a panoramic view of your life. You see the trail below and acknowledge that the winding road was treacherous and rocky, but from up here you can see the trip was worth the struggle. Your obstacles look small from the summit, and the panoramic view inspires you to begin charting new adventures.

How sad it is that I had to spend more than forty years of my life frustrated by my lack of direction. But that was my road. That was my rocky trail. And, there's a really important lesson to remember: without the obstacles, without the effort and pain, I would still be at basecamp.

When you remove blame as an option, you're free to see the good things in those past experiences. What do I mean? Well, let's take the year I got straight Ds as an example. Had I not earned the poor grades I deserved, I would not have seen the disappointment in my mother's eyes, or heard the cutting words from my brother: "What kind of idiot gets all Ds?" The pain that I felt was caused by my lack of effort. The result of that pain inspired me to change. Without the pain, I cannot say if I would have continued with that behavior or not. Sometimes we learn from our mistakes, and sometimes that's the only way we'll change.

Another example is that I frequently blamed my father for my lack of direction. For several years during my adolescence, he was gone for weeks at a time, when I needed guidance and a father figure. That wasn't fair to him; he had burdens, bills to pay and his own path to navigate. But he taught me to work hard and how to build things, and encouraged me to get into a skilled trade. Looking down from the mountain, I can see that trail (my lack of direction) actually presented me with numerous experiences that have enriched my life, and taught me about different people and occupations that I would have never experienced, had I not spent so many years chasing after God-knows-what. Bouncing from shoe shiner to laborer, to HVAC installer, to assembly worker, to pipefitter, to handyman, to house flipper, to writer, to blogger, to webmaster, to marathoner and sales professional are the very experiences that opened doors for me in other ways. My writing and experience in the trade led to a sales position. The sales position led me to learn more than I had ever imagined about business, people and mindset. Those learnings inspired me to write *The HVAC Millionaire Mindset*, a book that is now changing the lives of young men and women in the HVAC industry. That book led me to a mentor who encouraged me to join Toastmasters. Toastmasters led me to becoming an award-winning speaker in Indiana and Northern Kentucky. And that boost in self-confidence, coupled with my writing talents, led me to write this book. In the process, I've learned that the more people I serve, the more meaning I get in return. The more I impact the lives of others, the more purposeful my life becomes. This would not be possible without forgiving and taking ownership of my destiny.

The perspective that I am one hundred percent responsible for my life, choices and results is one of the key components that has freed me from the chains which once held me back. Wishing things were different is more toxic to my mindset than anything my parents did wrong. Forgiving them and freeing them from the responsibility of my faults and failures softened my heart, and giving them grace freed me to give grace to myself when I screw up, and grace to others when they harm me.

What about you? Who do you need to forgive and release from your chains? Who are you giving control of your life and choices to? It's time that you plant your flag in the ground and say: "From this point forward, in spite of where I came from, I now take one hundred percent responsibility to become the person required to accomplish my dreams."

Obviously, I don't know your story. Maybe one day I will. But I can tell you that you will love the view from the mountaintop, much more so than the cave. I can tell you, from experience, that when you release others from being responsible for your happiness, your success and your mindset, you will discover that becoming your greater purpose will take on a whole new meaning. Only then will you be truly free, to try the things you've been afraid to try, go after the career you always wanted and write the book that you've always dreamed of writing. When you're the only rock blocking your trail, it's much easier to clear the path, and to chisel and polish yourself. When there are others you think need to change, you never fix yourself, because you're too busy trying to polish the other rocks first, and changing other people isn't likely to happen. Ever.

Chapter 8

VISION

"Your vision will become clear only when you look into your heart.   Who looks outside, dreams.   Who looks inside awakens."

Carl Jung

After learning the importance of taking full responsibility, there were other lessons that turned my ship around. I learned that I need to figure out what I want and create a vision for my life. Look, I'm fifty-three years old at the time of this writing, and I'm not guaranteed another day (and neither are you, for that matter), so it's important that I'm as efficient as possible with my time, now more than ever. Taking one hundred percent responsibility for your life going forward is a good first step, but that's just the starting point.

Understanding "The Six Laws of Becoming" is essential if you want to find meaning and purpose in your life, because they all tie together, like individual strands in a rope. The more they twist together, the stronger they (and you) become.

Law #2: VISION
You must decide what you want.

Once you've decided to take one hundred percent responsibility to become the person required to reach your goals, you must then decide what you want. Until you know what you want to accomplish – your vision – you won't know what goals to set. Well, what if you don't know what you want? If you don't know right now, that's okay. We're all in different seasons of life. This may not be a visionary season for you; this may be a time for tilling the soil and clearing rocks. Sometimes we're simply living, fertilizing what's ahead. But, if now is the time for you to move forward, and you don't know what you want, you may need to think through your experiences, your ambitions and the many things you've wanted to accomplish during the various stages of your life. What commonalities do you see? Is there a pattern in your most memorable and exciting moments? Is there an experience that strikes a chord with you? Traveling? Relationships? Teaching? Helping? Adventure? Family? Mission work? Were there times when you served others that inspired you? When you're alone, is there a creative outlet that gives you energy? Painting? Writing? Singing? Building? Fixing? Creating? Programming? Speaking? Volunteering?

If it's difficult to identify what you want, that's perfectly normal. It took me over forty years of chasing until I knew exactly what I wanted to pursue. The goal is that you're living a life that's meaningful, and that you're striving for the things you want. It doesn't mean you have to turn your life upside down overnight; you may need time for reflection.

I suggest spending time alone to brainstorm, because you may want a lot of things that relate to different areas of your life. But, what's important is that you actively ask the question and put the answers in front of you, on paper, where you can review, edit and filter out the less important ideas.

The most simple method to figure out what you want is to write what you want followed by *"...because..."*. This exercise looks like this:

I want _____, *because* _____.

My answer looks like this:

"I want to teach mindset training to individuals and teams, because it makes me feel like my struggles and failures had a purpose ,and I want people to reach their full potential."

Now you try:

I want _ _ _ _ _ _ _ _ _ _ _ _ _ _ _ _ _, because _ _ _ _ _ _ _ _ _ _ _ _ _ _ _ _ _ _.

Repeat this several times. Do it with everything you want. After you have an exhaustive *"I want... because..."* list, you can evaluate which "wants" are more meaningful by the strength of their purpose.

If that exercise helps define what's important to you, practice writing a personal vision statement. Write several personal vision statements, using your *"I want... because..."* declarations, and eliminate the ones that feel less meaningful. Do this as many times as it takes, until you've created a vision you believe could legitimately guide your life choices – for now. Feel free to combine your most meaningful *"I want..."* statements if it makes sense. It doesn't have to be perfect or permanent; starting the process is what's important.

Once you have a working personal vision statement that defines what you want from life, you can begin using it to guide your thoughts, choices, actions and results. This is an important step because, if you're faced with an activity that requires a significant amount of time, resources or commitment from you, that does not align with your vision statement, you'll have a guide to determine if you really want to do it. A vision statement will steer you in the right direction.

A personal vision statement should define what you want your life to look like, determine how you spend your time, structured around your values, and establish what you want to focus on. Of course, you'll need to balance your current obligations and relationships with your vision, so don't neglect your other responsibilities. The point is to take some time and focus on your vision, away from distractions, so you can get clarity.

When writing your vision statement, plan for "life" to happen. There will be bumps in the road but, now that you have a growth mindset, you understand that setbacks are opportunities to learn. So, be flexible and avoid rigid expectations. Roll with the curveballs that life throws, and use your vision as a tool to bring you back into focus. Once you establish your vision, expect to revise it over time, to more closely reflect your values and goals, because these evolve through the seasons of life.

You see, you can't flip a switch and suddenly find your greater purpose; *Oops! There it is!* There's your purpose, hiding under the cushions of the couch, amidst the pennies and popcorn. No, that's not how it works. The reason I told all of those stories, earlier in this book, is for you to understand how important the entirety of your life is to your greater purpose, because it's your story that's made you. So, if you've not taken time to reflect on your life – the good, the bad and the ugly – you should reread the previous chapters, spend some time releasing anyone that you are still holding accountable to your growth going forward, and get a better understanding of who you are. Sometimes, the messy parts of your life can help other people who've gone through a similar mess. Sometimes, the challenges you've overcome have equipped you to help others with the same problems.

Unforgiveness is a bottleneck to becoming your greater purpose and discovering what you want. So, if this is really difficult for you, take a couple of steps back and investigate if there's someone you haven't released from your past. If you're still letting someone have control of your life and choices, and the direction you want to go, you may find it very difficult to move forward. So, start with forgiveness. This is why taking one hundred percent responsibility is an important first step.

Release. Forgive. Take a hundred responsibility from this point forward, only then will you be free to build the future you desire.

Many people pondered their significance during the dark hours of COVID, and began searching for meaning, for the first time, or once again after a long, dry spell. As the world was crumbling apart, and we were locked down with our families, life came to a sudden halt. For the first time in many years, we were forced to slow down, if not completely stop running the rat race. During this time, I thought about my existence, and I started asking questions that I hadn't asked before, like, what am I doing with my life? Do I want to keep doing my job? Have I done anything meaningful? What's this been about, anyway? Life was on pause because of the pandemic. I was forced to slow down, and I finally had time to think. Looking back, I can see how important that was for me.

If you haven't stepped away from your hectic life, you might consider doing so, because there's tremendous value in quiet solitude. I believe that's why so many of us found ourselves pondering our existence, meaning and purpose during the COVID outbreak: we had no choice. I think we instinctively do that when we're removed from life's circus. Times like that force us to consider our mortality and our legacy. I thought about my family and what I'd leave behind, if the big C were to take me. I did this for many days. While the world was on a hard pause, and the phone was no longer ringing, I sat in my home office, thinking. It felt really good to be moving at a snail's pace, because I had been moving at the speed of light for years. I thought about each of my children, my wife, my work, my interests and my spiritual beliefs. I started asking what I wanted for each of those compartments in my life and, if I lived, how would I go forward? *What's really important to me? How can I make a difference with the time I have left?* I asked myself. *How will I work to accomplish those desires? What will guide me and hold me accountable to attaining the new standards I am creating for myself?* And I wondered how I'd do this so that it makes sense, in a way that doesn't just fizzle out as soon as work ramps up again.

It started with a piece of paper, as do most good ideas. Writing my thoughts has always been a great starting point – maybe this will work for you, too. Write the following subjects at the top of a blank piece of paper:

RELATIONSHIPS:

CAREER:

PERSONAL WANTS:

FINANCES:

HEALTH:

LONG-TERM GOALS:

SPIRITUAL:

Write everything that comes to mind when you think about those areas of your life. What can you do to add meaning to you and others? When do you feel most fulfilled? What is the best part of each category? What inspires you the most in that area of your life? What gets you fired up?

Start with your relationships, then do this with all of the other areas of your life: finances, hobbies, your talents, your career, your health, your spiritual beliefs. Once you have an exhaustive list of your hopes and dreams, circle a few of the words that stick out to you as the most important in each category. Write several keywords under each category and create a concise vision statement, using all of your keywords in one sentence. Plan to erase, scrap and delete often. This is just an exercise, not a final exam. If you don't like what you've come up with, get a fresh sheet of paper and start over.

This might feel uncomfortable. If you're like most people, your life is moving non-stop, so pausing to reflect on your life, and think about where you are and where you're going, may feel awkward. But that's okay; you're becoming your greater purpose, and this is part of the process, a process that requires you to think deeply about what's important to you, and about bringing a higher level of meaning. So, the time you spend doing this will be well worth it. You might even discover that you're doing exactly what you should be doing. Sometimes, we get so caught up in the struggles of life that we take our life for granted, and forget that we're already doing what's most important to us. So, contemplating our vision can serve as a pleasant reminder of the joy we're already experiencing, but too busy to acknowledge.

If you're still having trouble figuring out what you want, consider watching the TED talk by Dr. Hugo Kehr.[12] Dr. Kehr, Chair of Psychology at the Technical University of Munich, Germany, gave a talk on what motivates people. In his talk, he explains that there are essentially three aspects of our lives that, when tied together, give us meaning and motivate us to accomplish our biggest ambitions. The three components of motivation are MIND, HEART and HAND.

- *MIND* is the idea that what you are doing is important. Does your vision logically make sense and is it really making a difference?

- *HEART* is the idea that what you're doing is something you enjoy. It's something you know adds value and meaning to your life, and you feel it emotionally.

- *HAND* means that it's a skill you have, or one that you can develop, if the skill is needed to match the motivation in your heart and mind.

Now you fill in the MIND, HAND and HEART parts of your life. Like all of the exercises, repeat as often as necessary.

- *MIND:* What are you doing now, and/or want to do, that you feel is important? Is it really making a difference? Does it positively impact other people?

- *HEART:* What are you doing now, and/or want to do, that adds value and meaning to you?

- *HAND:* What skills do you have (or can develop), that contribute to your HEART and MIND objectives?

Taken from seventeenth-century Swiss educator Johann Pestalozzi's research, Kehr states that these three elements are the components that create "flow" – that feeling you get when you are so caught up in your work that time flies by and you're in a zone, and whatever you're doing is so enjoyable that it feels effortless. This is how I feel when I'm writing or creating content, or helping others develop. So, if you're struggling to define what you want, maybe looking at the MIND, HEART and HAND components can help you discover a vision for your life.

In the book, *The On-Purpose Person,* Kevin W. McCarthy suggests using a tournament bracket as a tool to discover what's most meaningful to you. When listing all the things you want by category (relationships, finance, career, health, etc.), you can use the brackets to eliminate the categories that you're less passionate about. I like this idea, but I think it could exclude aspects of your life that you don't want to leave behind. For example, if family and relationships win the championship, many people don't want to leave faith, finances or health out of their vision. So, try using the tournament bracket to find out what is most important in the major categories of your life, and then create a vision statement that encapsulates all of your winners in a single vision.

In his book, *How to Develop Your Personal Mission Statement,* Stephen R. Covey suggests building your mission statement around the "ends" and the "means". The intent of this exercise is to include your destination and the "how" to get there in your vision. I do this, but I separate the two. I have a vision statement and a "mode"; the mode is my "how", the way I build the future I envision. Your personal mission statement, according to Covey, is: *"Who you really are, and what you could become."*[13]

I'm sure you can find other creative ways to discover and refine your vision. It's important to get started. It's not rocket science; play around, and revise as needed.

Knowing where you're going is critical to becoming your greater purpose because, without a clearly stated vision, you'll end up somewhere, but it might not be where you want to go. This is why your vision is so important: it's a guide. It's a roadmap. It's the arrow on your compass, pointing you in the right direction. Bryan Tracey, speaker, coach and bestselling author, said: "A clear vision, backed by definite plans, gives you a tremendous feeling of confidence and personal power."

This is definitely true for me. As a writer, one of the questions people ask me is: "How do you come up with all those ideas and put them together, into a book?" The answer is actually pretty simple: the idea, like any good idea, just pops into my head unexpectedly. This happens to everyone. But I've learned that it's important to write the idea down, so that it doesn't get lost or forgotten. Once I have a premise for a book, I write it in my little book of ideas. I then make a simple outline, showing each step it will take to bring my protagonist from where he starts to where he transforms into the person required to be the hero. And this is how you can cast your personal vision: the idea starts in your head – you see an image of where you want to go – then you write it down and build it out, step by step. The process of outlining a novel is exactly the same process you can use to build the life you want. Resist letting the feeling of being overwhelmed over take you. Do it step by step.

If you ever watched the Mel Gibson film, *Braveheart*, you might remember the scene where William Wallace, played by Gibson, storms into the battlelines on his horse, with blue warpaint on his face, and gives a motivational speech that inspires his fellow countrymen to win the battle. It's a memorable scene and the movie was great, but it all started on a piece of paper, when Mel Gibson and Randall Wallace began with a simple vision. And that vision was cast by writing a script, broken down into individual scenes and individual lines of dialogue, one word at a time. All Mel and Randall did was create their vision with words – and you can do the same. With their vision in front of them, they were able to build the movie, one scene at a time. They evaluated the vision and carefully built on each component. They wrote the script, hired actors and skilled individuals to build the set, created a musical score and wardrobe, then filmed it in an appropriate setting. *Badaboom, badabing! Braveheart!* You can do the same with your life! You are the writer, director and producer. You have creative control. What do you want your life's movie to look like? Don't think about what it takes to create the entire film (your final destination); focus on one component at at time. First, write the script (your vision). Next, create the wardrobe (traits & skills you will need). Then build the set (the logistics — website, build a savings, get a new job, etc). Then, add the musical score and make up (the details). This is your life. Build it to match your vision.

Joseph Campbell said, "A dream is your creative vision for your life in the future." So get creative. Don't put any limits on your vision. Let your imagination run wild, and build a vision for your life where there are no limitations to what's possible. You can hone-in on the details and set manageable goals later.

My vision statement started out as: *"I help my family and customers get what they want, and help as many people along the way."* In time, it became: *"Positively helping individuals and teams get what they want."* That statement came from my story, my faith, my family, my desire to serve, and my desire to help people get what they want. It covers all my bases (family, spiritual life, career goals, finances, desire to make a difference, etc.). After multiple revisions, it states very clearly where I'm going and how I set my priorities. Today, my vision statement is very concise: *"Positively helping teams and individuals get what they want, reach their full potential and become their greater purpose."*

I do this by focusing on the following statement, which I call my "mode": the how; the way I live out my vision. How do I live out that vision? By "purposefully dreaming, responsibly developing, focusing and taking action." And this is where "The Six Laws of Becoming" play off each other: by establishing what I want, and taking one-hundred percent responsibility to become the person capable of accomplishing my vision, I begin to make goals, break them down into manageable steps, get laser-focused and take action.

When you begin to follow "The Six Laws of Becoming", you'll discover that you have some habits that get in the way. Changing habits (physical and mental) and learning new skills is the developmental part. Once you have a vision, and you begin working toward making that happen, you'll discover that there are other obstacles that get in your way: time, financial, red tape, qualifications, etc.

And that's why the next law is so important, because, without a definite purpose or strong reason for your vision, your dream could begin to fizzle out at the first sign of trouble. I don't want that. You don't want that. So, let's dive into the *WHY* that will fuel your vision.

Chapter 9

PURPOSE

"The great men and women of history were not great because of what they earned and owned, but rather for what they gave their lives to accomplish."

John C. Maxwell

Taking one hundred percent responsibility to become the person capable of fulfilling your vision is a critical first step, and creating a vision gives clarity to where you want to go. But, as you may have already discovered, life is hard and riddled with challenges. Relationships, as meaningful as they are, can create conflict. Industries and careers come and go, economies rise and fall, and our health and safety is never guaranteed. So, what reason would you have to do what you want, if this is your last day? What is your *why*? Why is this thing that you want (your vision or goal) the most important thing in the world to you? Your reason – your *why*, your purpose – must be so important that, come hell or high water, mountain or valley, or death and dismemberment, you must do it. That's what a greater purpose looks like, and you are becoming it. You've been becoming this greater purpose your entire life. Now that you've reflected on what you want, it's time to discover why you want it. It's time to put a label on it.

Law #3: PURPOSE
Find the reason for your vision.

A purpose is the reason you get out of bed, and it is the ambition that undergirds your strengths and passions. This should be the underlining focus of your vision. For me, my vision is to help individuals and teams discover their greater purpose. I want folks to uncover their full potential with mindset training, because this process reveals the holes and weaknesses that have been preventing them from getting what they want. I'm passionate about teaching this, because I spent so much of my life aimlessly trying to figure out who I am and where I'm going, that once I discovered I can actually take control of my life and steer it in the direction that I want to go, I was like: *What the hell? Why didn't I hear this growing up?* Mindset training is so simple, and can be taught in a one-hour talk or a half-day seminar, yet we don't teach it in most families, schools, colleges or businesses. When I discovered what was holding me back, and began teaching others how to get what they want, I realized that this isn't something I *can* do; this is something I *must* do!

Teaching mindset training is so important to me that I want to share this message with anyone who wants to hear it, because I want everyone to reach their full potential and discover their greater purpose. It's important for you to learn why you were created for such a time as this, because you will experience greater joy, fulfillment and peace when you understand how you fit into the puzzle of life. Understanding this about yourself brings us all closer to each other, closer to God, closer to the world around us, and builds empathy for anyone who has gone through similar struggles.

But that's me. That's *my* aspiration. And it's taken decades for me to become this person. It's taken decades of struggling for me to get here. And, now that I know what I know, I have to remain vigilant, or I will slip right back into my old ways.

Becoming your greater purpose takes intention. If you're not conscious of what you're becoming, you could become someone you're not happy with. If you're not living with a greater purpose, you could be living with a lesser purpose. If you find yourself in a place where you're going through the motions, with zero passion, push the pause button and block out some time to reflect on what you actually want from life, and what you really care about.

If you can find meaning and purpose in what you're doing now, that's great! You may become re-energized and reignite that spark you once had. If not, life is short; no point spending your valuable time becoming miserable, and doing something that gives you no sense of purpose. If this is the case, try using the MIND, HEART and HAND exercise discussed in the previous chapter, to help you find a greater purpose. Discovering what puts you in the flow state will help in discovering your passion and purpose as well.

Your *why* is so important, not simply because it has become a cliche of sorts – partly due to Simon Sinek's book, *Start with Why* – but because we all need an internal motivation to get our gears moving. A practical example of this is when your bills are due. You get up in the morning to go to work, even if it's doing something you hate, because you're motivated by the fear of debt collectors, a bad credit score and bankruptcy. Therefore, you wake up, often begrudgingly, from the force of a loud and aggravating alarm clock. The less motivated you are, the more you hit the snooze. And yet you wake up and go to work.

Without those forces (fear and aggravation), we'd lie in bed, go hungry, become homeless and go into debt. These are nothing more than incentives, to accomplish the most basic act of stepping out of bed, then stepping into the shower, throwing down some coffee and going to work. Now, if you can do that, and still manage to live a relatively comfortable, relatively happy and relatively normal life, just imagine what kind of energy you'd have if you had a much stronger purpose; a deeper motivation; an incredibly exciting reason to go after your vision and take action to reach your goals, and pursue something you love beyond life.

Imagine living your vision. Close your eyes and see it happening in your mind. What are you doing? What does a typical day in that world look like? Who are the lives that you touch? How will you make a difference? In what ways will their lives change, as a result of you deciding to take a bold step to accomplish your vision?

In this chapter, you will dig deep into your vision and the passion you have for making that dream a reality. This is where you will find your *why*. If your vision is to make the lives of others better, by sharing your story, focus on the joy and hope that they will receive because your message communicates that they are not alone, and that change is possible. If your vision is to create a product that makes a task easier, think of your customers, and the joy they will feel because someone took a risk, and invested in something that made the world a better place. If your vision is to become rich, save lives, travel the world, serve the homeless, rescue animals, grow your company, inspire others, get fit, feed the poor, clean up your community, spread a message of hope, or any worthy pursuit, there is transformational power within. If this is the case, your vision is coming from the right place: your MIND, HEART and HAND.

Too often, we're looking for what we get out of our vision, and that's a valid concern. If your vision will become your livelihood, you must take that into account. If your vision is not an instrument for building wealth, because that is not a concern for you, you'll have to structure your lifestyle to accommodate a lower income. If that's where your heart is, that shouldn't be a problem for you; living frugally and simply are not difficult when you're passionate about what you do. However, when your passions require money and travel and time, it will be important that you keep your eye on the prize. You must keep your focus on the reason you started your venture, or your passion could wane.

If your passion is a side hustle financed by your day job, your biggest obstacle will be keeping balance. So, I recommend pursuing your vision on the side, or integrating it into your career over quitting your job. I think it's a good idea to let your work support your vision until the vision can support you. Don't quit your day job while the flower is taking root; go full-time when the flower is ready to bloom.

Creating a strong purpose will have more meaning if it's less about you. In fact, if you can remove yourself from your vision statement altogether, and point that vision in the direction of others, you will get more energy to accomplish it. Over time, you learn that true joy comes from serving and helping others. I got through the hard stuff in my life and learned many life lessons, some of which are that serving myself is a short-lived pleasure, but serving others in service to my creator gives me an incredible sense of fulfillment.

I'm at peace with who I am now, and I'm more fulfilled when I inspire someone else to reach their full potential. I get double the energy when someone else's life is better, than when I'm serving myself. But I'm not talking about self-denigration, either; you can be passionate about others and still work toward financial freedom and wealth, with goals in multiple areas of your life. A heart for service and helping others runs parallel with success. The more people you help, the greater success you'll experience, period. You can see it in any individual or organization passionately pursuing their mission. Service and success are a cause and effect; when service of any kind is the cause, success, meaning and purpose are the effects.

Ed Mylett teaches five keys to uncover your purpose, in one of his YouTube videos.[14] The five keys will help you think about your life and meaning. They'll help you break down some of your misconceptions about what a greater purpose "has to be", and help stimulate some ideas. Take a few minutes and consider each key. I have added my commentary on each point, to encourage additional reflection.

- *KEY #1: Your purpose doesn't have to be your occupation.*

  Great point! Many people have become their greater purpose through volunteer work, side hustles, teaching, coaching, mentoring or training others. Engineers passionate about robotics have trained thousands of youngsters in local robotics clubs, in their free time. Every community has an army of men and women that coach our kids, by developing commitment and discipline through sports. They volunteer or get paid very little. I've been building *The Mindset Mission* for two years, at the time of this writing. It started when I began training my customers and their techs with mindset training. Out of that passion I wrote *The HVAC Millionaire Mindset,* and have devoted countless hours to researching, reading, and preparing my presentations and speaking skills, so that I can develop myself for increased service. Passions can become your career, but your purpose can also be the thing that is supported by your day job. And, it's possible that pursuing your greater purpose on the side can stimulate a greater passion in your career, too.

- *KEY #2: Your "calling" will always involve helping others.*

  Reiterating the point I made previously, if you're looking for meaning in your life, it can certainly be found in helping other people. Can you experience joy by pursuing the things that only make you happy? Sure you can. Mauro Morandi lived alone on the island of Budelli, off the coast of northern Italy, for nearly 33 years, and he was happy. But what kind of life is that? It's definitely not for everyone. Long-lasting joy and a sense of purpose come from helping people you can relate to, or have a natural sense of empathy toward.

- *KEY #3: Your calling will involve your natural talents.*

  Spot on, Ed! Your natural gifts are exactly that: gifts. We all have them, and that's part of becoming: discovering who you are, why you're here, and finding the gifts that you've been given, so that you can make the contribution to the world you were created for. Stretching yourself, pushing the boundaries of your capabilities and having diverse experiences will help you find those talents and gifts.

- *KEY #4: Try new things.*

  Ed encourages his listeners to try a side hustle. Try starting a micro-business. Try volunteering in your area of interest. There's no rush; you don't have to have your greater purpose figured out by the end of this book. Make a plan to discover something new every weekend for the next year, and see what you come up with. Experience as much of the world as you can, and eventually something will stick. When you find that thing you're passionate about, you'll know it. And, if it feels like you're trying, but nothing gels with you, keep exploring. Don't give up. Remember the *YET* principle from your growth mindset: you haven't found it *yet!* Your greater purpose is found in the searching, so keep moving. You're gonna have some great stories to tell.

- *KEY #5: What would you do if you had all the time in the world?*

  We addressed this earlier. Think about what you would do if time and money weren't an issue. What would bring you lasting joy? Be creative; don't put any boundaries on the possibilities. Go for a walk, where the best ideas are discovered, and let your imagination run wild. Don't forget to write down every idea you come up with. Start taking action on those ideas; try them out and test the waters. And remember that without change, without thinking differently, everything will stay the same. So, don't hope for purpose; develop and work to change yourself, and you just might find that a new perspective on life is what you needed.

Your purpose is deeply personal, so get out there and experience life on your terms. The point is to get out of your comfort zone, to get a new perspective. And remember that becoming your greater purpose is not about a single journey; *it's the entire journey of your life*.

The power of contemplation.

It's important to understand that the act of thinking about your purpose is powerful enough to improve the way you approach daily challenges. Even if you don't nail down your *why* just yet, thinking about it will improve your life.

In an article written by Jackie Swift, in the *Research and Innovation* blog, by The University of Cornell, she points out a study by Anthony L. Burrow, from the university's College of Human Ecology. In the study, a group of college students were split into two groups; one group wrote about their purpose for five minutes, and the other group were told to write about the most recent film they had watched. Then, the students rode the north-south train, from end to end, and were instructed to journal their mood and emotions as they traveled.

Researchers know from previous studies that humans get uneasy the farther they get away from their ethnic and racial group. What Burrow discovered was that the students who wrote about the movie began to feel anxious and uncomfortable, as new ethnic and racial groups boarded the train. This was expected. However, the study found that: *"Those who had written about their sense of purpose had a different outcome. 'They were emotionally even-keel,' Burrow says. 'Their mood was not contingent on the population of the passengers around them. This is one of the things we believe a sense of purpose affords us: it gives a sense of psychological homeostasis. We are confronted with the ups and downs of life, but purpose is an active ingredient that helps us stay stable.'"*[15]

Intentionally formulating a purpose, to guide your vision and goals, will not only make life more enjoyable, but it will give you a sense of stability. Time and experiences are the things that have made you who you are today. As time goes on, you'll expand your horizons and become someone different, through the many seasons of your life. Yes, there's a maturing process, but becoming aware of and searching for meaning in those experiences will add much more value to your heart than just going through the motions.

The power in purpose.

Becoming your greater purpose is a process, and life is filled with challenges, so don't think that having a purpose going forward will make everything easy; that's farthest from the truth. Having a greater purpose will not change the realities of life. Life will not change for you. The challenge is for you to change, so you can more easily adapt to the difficulties of life when they arise – and they will; there are struggles ahead. You will experience loss. You will experience heartache. In the words of Jim Rohn, there will always be springs, summers, falls and winters; the seasons of life will not change. Becoming your greater purpose will not make problems go away, but it will help you to remain grounded when problems come to the surface. And, if you have a strong faith in a higher power, that, too, can ground you when life gets messy. Your purpose will help you remain focused, in spite of the distractions and noise of life – and there will be many. Nothing is easy.

Big dreams consist of mountains to cross, stormy seas to navigate and difficulties of all kinds. Whether you pursue a greater purpose, or live with no meaning whatsoever, you will still contend with the ups and downs of living. But, when you encounter gale forces on your journey, having a lighthouse to guide the way will make all the difference in whether you crash against the rocks or land safely on shore.

Anne Lamott once said: "Lighthouses don't go running all around an island, looking for a boat to save; they just stand there, shining." And that's what a greater purpose in your life will do for you: it will guide your way through the storms of life, like a lighthouse, giving you something to focus on when you feel like the waves are going to overturn your ship. This is one of the reasons so many people fail at keeping their new year resolutions: they don't have a strong enough reason to maintain the disciplines needed to accomplish their goals. Resolutions are usually pretty self-centered, like losing weight to look better, and that's why we fail. But those who decide to change because their lifestyle is killing them are truly motivated to change. Changing for vanity's sake doesn't seem to cut it. Changing because you've got something really important to accomplish has more power.

The Dalai Lama said: "Our prime purpose in life is to help others. And, if you can't help them, at least don't hurt them." T.D. Jakes wrote: *"If you can't figure out your purpose, figure out your passion. For your passion will lead you right into your purpose."* This is why I believe that defining your vision (deciding what you want) is a critical step. Once you know what you want, which is likely something you are passionate about, it's a good idea to uncover the reason for that passion. And I love what the Buddha said about your purpose: "Your purpose in life is to find your purpose, and give your whole heart and soul to it."

If you still need help finding your why, work through the *"I want... because..."* exercise you did while working on your vision statement. State what you want and follow up with *"because..."* Previously, the goal was to discover what you want by attaching a sense of meaning to that desire; this time, the focus is on *why* you want it. There's a good chance that you'll eliminate some of the things you thought you wanted, when you discover the reason you want it is superficial, or not as meaningful as you thought.

Do this exercise several times today, and then again a few days later:

I want _____, *because* _____.

Your purpose is the power behind your vision. If your vision is the roadmap that leads you where you want to go, your purpose is the rocket fuel that will propel you forward. Your purpose will give you clarity in every aspect of your life. It will give you permission to participate in some activities, and prevent you from participating in activities that pull you away from what you want. Your greater purpose is tied to your values, and will dictate how you spend your time, what habits you choose to keep and what habits you need to stop.

Your greater purpose should revolve around your vision like a moon orbiting the Earth. Your vision is the nucleus, and your greater purpose is the electron that gives it energy; it helps you manage the tides and seasons of your life. It inhabits your moral compass, motivations and goals.

Your greater purpose should reflect the meaning that you have uncovered through all of your trials and tribulations. Your greater purpose should be representative of not only who you are at this moment, but who you're becoming, because you are becoming more than a single moment in time, more than a memory, more than a painful experience, more than your age, more than a single accomplishment and more than net worth. You are becoming the person you were designed to become, through a lifetime of challenges that, as a result, have made you the only person uniquely qualified to be you.

In the article, "The Science of Living With Purpose", by Claire Gauen, she cites Patrick Hill, Associate Professor of Psychological and Brain Sciences, at Washington University in St. Louis, when she states: *"Purpose imparts direction and structure to both daily life and long-term plans. Across numerous populations, age ranges and geographic locations, an overarching theme remains: 'Having a sense of purpose seems to be valuable for health and well-being.'"*[16]

There are other studies which show that your health, longevity and joy, in even the smallest tasks in daily life, are more meaningful if you're living with purpose. In fact, there are healing powers in becoming your greater purpose. In the article, "The Science Behind the Powerful Benefits of Having a Purpose", by Majid Fotuhi, MD, Ph.D. and Sara Mehr, there are many studies mentioned that have shown incredible improvement in patients suffering from cognitive decline, due to Alzheimer's, strokes, sleep apnea and frailty. The authors summarize the article by stating: *"Clearly, having a purpose in life is a powerful tool that can improve the quality of life for our patients, and lessen the burden of several chronic medical conditions in our society."*[17]

When you forgive, and take one hundred percent responsibility for your choices and results, you're free to become the person you're meant to become. And, when you find a powerful purpose for your vision, you will have the motivation to get it done. However, you must also take very specific steps to get there. In any journey, you need a map (vision), fuel (purpose) and guideposts (goals).

We must not forget each point along the way, because you can't travel long distances on a single tank of gas. You need to plan your trip with several manageable and strategically placed goals, throughout the journey. These stops along your path generate excitement and a sense of accomplishment. They refuel your engine and let you stretch your legs. Therefore, setting goals and getting laser-focused on them is the next step to getting what you want and reaching your full potential. As you progress on your journey, and consider the greater purpose for your vision, I hope you're getting some ideas about where you're heading, and how you plan to get there.

Chapter 10

FOCUS

"Concentrate all your thoughts upon the work at hand. The sun's rays do not burn until brought to a focus."

Alexander Graham Bell

Setting and achieving goals is hard. When you don't reach a goal you set for yourself, you feel like a failure, and it discourages you from trying again. This is a pretty common occurrence; I know this oh too well. In fact, in the article "Why People Fail to Achieve Their Goals", by Douglas Vermeenen,[18] he concludes that there are ten reasons why people miss the mark. Vermeenen states that, if you can overcome your mistakes, you can become anything you want. I have to agree with him. He notes that about eighty percent of people don't make any goals of significance and, of the twenty percent that actually set goals, most aren't stretching goals that are very challenging at all. Yet, seventy percent of those who set goals still fail to achieve their objective. Vermeenen assembled the list below, stating why we tend to fail to reach our goals:

1. Fear of success or failure.
2. Lack of knowledge in goal-setting tactics.
3. Lack of commitment.
4. Inactivity.
5. Analysis paralysis.
6. Lack of purpose.

7. Lack of planning.
8. Too many goals.
9. Sense of unworthiness.
10. Lack of motivation.

The truth is, until I started writing I knew very little about setting goals. I think the idea of setting goals is commonly understood, because we hear it so often growing up. We hear the word "goals" all the time, in sports and at work, but when we're young, we're not given the framework for plotting and accomplishing goals. Our basic understanding is that a goal is a target to reach, but the mechanics are rarely discussed. And yet, goal-setting and achievement have been studied at great length, and we have a pretty good idea of how anyone can achieve practically anything they set their mind to, when they follow a goal-setting process.

In this chapter, we'll discuss why it's important to learn the art of goal-setting and focus. After you've committed to taking one hundred percent responsibility to become the person capable of accomplishing your dream, designed your vision for what you want from life, and established the greater purpose for that vision, you have to start building the roadmap to make it happen. And, it's important to learn how to map your life; if you can do this successfully, you can do it over and over, as the seasons of life change.

Truth is, there is no end game until you take your last breath. Becoming your greater purpose is ongoing. Your vision can change. Desires and values can evolve as you move through the many stages of your life. So, when life changes course, you want to have the skills required to navigate to a new destination. And, if you're embarking on a new challenge, as a result of this book, you need to understand the fourth law of becoming:

Law #4: FOCUS
Get laser-focused on your goals.

In all fairness, goal-setting is intuitive to some people. Many athletes and high-performing students have used goals to hit their next target, reaching for a specific weight they want to bench press, or speed they want to run for the mile, or vertical jump, or earn a specific GPA. I learned to set goals by running and writing, two disciplines that demand I set and reach my goals.

When I was in college, I would read *Runner's World* magazine and study the training regimens of the world's best runners. I couldn't run at their distances or times, but I would shrink their world-class workouts to my skill level. If they ran ten 1,000-meter sprints, I'd run five. If they ran a twelve-mile easy run, I'd run six. If they did ladders going from 400 to 800, to 1600, to 3200-meter, up-tempo speed work, I'd create a smaller version of that workout. One thing I learned during that time was that having the featured runner's weekly plan visually in front of me made it so much easier to hit my goals. On Monday, I'd wake up and look at the page I cut out of the magazine, then I would just do fifty percent of that workout.

Keeping that paper tacked onto the little bulletin board in my bedroom made all the difference. I'd see the full-page picture of the runner, which motivated me, because they were in perfect shape and wearing all the best running clothes. The adjoining page displayed the workout: Monday, Tuesday, Wednesday, rest day, Friday, Saturday, Sunday. The week was laid out perfectly, explaining in detail how far, how fast, and whether it was a road run, trail or track workout. This made it much easier to stick to the plan, because all I had to do was take orders, and I was good at that. I may not have been the most disciplined person on the planet but, looking back at my strengths back then, I was a hard worker. So, if someone could point me in the right direction and tell me where to go, I'd do it and work hard at it – just give me a to-do list, so that I could check off each accomplishment. These pre-planned workouts did the trick.

This carried over, many years later, when I was learning how to train for a marathon. I had to study the process, because training for a race that pushes your physical and mental capacity beyond its limit requires planning. Being the bull-headed person that I am, I did very little research for my first marathon and I paid the price. I overtrained early on, wreaking havoc on my body, causing many injuries that, in the end, left me unprepared to go beyond eighteen miles without suffering the typical pains and dehydration mistakes beginners make. I barely finished my first marathon, by walking and jogging with severe pain in my knees, and cramping in every muscle group due to dehydration. I was a disaster.

My foray into running marathons was poorly planned and not timed well. I didn't have a specific time I wanted to hit, because I just wanted to find out if I could go the distance. Yes, I finished, but I didn't reach my full potential, because I put in an average effort in terms of gaining knowledge about the required training. In other words, I broke the cardinal laws of goal-setting, based on the famous acronym *SMART*, created by George Doran, Arthur Miller and James Cunningham, back in the early eighties.

SMART GOALS:

S = Specific

M = Measurable

A = Attainable

R = Realistic

T = Time-bound

For decades, corporations and coaches have used this architecture to help individuals and teams reach their goals. It's proven and effective. When you set very specific goals and simplify them into smaller, manageable steps with a completion date, you have a much higher chance of reaching that goal, as long as it's an achievable, realistic goal. We also know that we perform better when our goals push us to our limits.

If reaching goals is so easy, why do so few people set and accomplish goals?

It seems that the lack of goal accomplishment is rooted in very personal issues. Fear of success or failure is a deep-seated fear, that may run over into many aspects of our lives. The fear of success and failure will impact your career, finances and relationships. But, it's a mindset problem: fear of success and failure reflects a fixed mindset. This, however, can be overcome by rewiring how you view success and failure, by doing the exercises in the previous chapters, and by taking the *30-Day Mindset Challenge* I'll discuss at the end of the book. By forming a growth mindset, you'll reaffirm that success comes with effort and the power of *yet.* By building a growth mindset, you understand that failure is part of the process, not a debilitating problem. So, if you address your mindset first, these fears can be laid to rest. Fear is normal. Failure is normal. In fact, failure is good, because that's where you learn the most important lessons. How you address those fears and failures is part of your becoming.

Lack of knowledge on goal-setting tactics is an easy fix: simply read and learn. Discover the best goal-setting tools that work for you. The *SMART* goal-setting technique is a universal method, but there are some really great books that you can read on goal-setting, by Brian Tracy, Zig Ziggler, Jim Rohn, Richard Koch and many more. And there are great podcasts and TED talks that can help you, too. Just Google *"goal-setting TED talks"*, and you can learn the art of goal-setting in no time. Use the supercomputer attached to your hip and download the data to your brain. And, if you want to start changing faster, read Mel Robbins's book, *The 5 Second Rule.* We're not living in the dark ages; there's no reason you can't learn efficient ways of setting and reaching goals in our modern age. Not taking the steps needed to reach your goals is a problem you can fix. A quick read of a book or two, and half a dozen videos, will nearly make you an expert, if you follow up with action and repetition.

Lack of commitment could also be a problem. Circling back to finding your *why*, a definite purpose or reason for your vision will cure a lack of commitment, if your goal is truly something you want. Why do you want it? Why must you do it? If you don't have a strong enough reason, maybe you shouldn't be wasting your time. However, if you know that your goal is really important for you to accomplish, the time you spend discovering your *why* may be the key to getting over the lack-of-commitment problem. This is why we focus on "The Six Laws of Becoming": they all play off each other, impact many areas of your life and guide you toward reaching your vision.

My goal to run my first marathon was vague, because I only wanted to know if I could finish. I knew when it was going to take place, but I didn't invest the time needed to learn how to measure my progress. I didn't know how to properly train, or how to increase my endurance, without causing overuse injuries. When I completed that first marathon, and experienced the excitement of accomplishing a big goal, and checking that off my bucket list, I was eager for the next challenge: qualifying for the Boston Marathon. Accomplishing that goal required a very specific time for my age group, and it would require a very specific training regimen. Once I set a specific time goal (running the marathon in 3 hours, 25 minutes), I began learning how to properly train, mapped out a training schedule, about six months in advance, highlighted the distances I needed for the progressively increasing long runs, week after week, and planned a two-week taper period, prior to the race. Then, I just did the individual workouts, one at a time, and rested on the days I had planned. I hit all the milestones, and could run nearly twenty miles at race pace when I entered a race in Charlevoix, Michigan, in 2015. Unfortunately, I didn't have enough gas in the tank; I came within less than a minute of qualifying that summer day. It took two more tries until I finally did it, in November of 2016. That goal was accomplished because it was specific, measurable, attainable, realistic and time-bound. Yes, it took several tries, and I had to make adjustments around injuries and family activities, but that's how failing and effort works: you make a mistake and try again. No big deal. Fail and learn.

The *SMART* goal-setting process works. It creates a roadmap that you can follow. Without specific goals and milestones to measure progress, you don't know if you're really on track. I love what Brian Tracy said: "If you don't know where you are going, you'll end up someplace else." Motivational speaker and author Denis Waitley said: "The reason most people never reach their goals is that they don't define them, or ever seriously consider them as believable or achievable. Winners can tell you where they are going, what they plan to do along the way, and who will be sharing the adventure with them."

Don't look at goal-setting as a method for only hitting big milestones, or achieving an income or a bucket list. Goal-setting works the same way when planning any objective, like writing a novel: you start with an idea, write it down on paper, and begin breaking your concept into a progression of plot twists that bring your protagonist through a dramatic change process. Along the way you develop characters, giving them obstacles to overcome and opportunities for change; there are always conflict and opportunities for growth. Step by step, the protagonist moves closer to their greater purpose. Sometimes you have to scratch a chapter and start over; sometimes you have to "kill your darlings", as they say. If you're an experienced writer, you can even plan a completion date, if you know how many words you can write per day.

It's important to know that reaching your goals is easier when you take your focus off the big picture from time to time, and focus on the smaller components. Once you map your path to reach each goal, don't focus on the final results, or everything needed to accomplish it, simply focus on the individual steps that you laid out in advance. Keep your focus on the smaller projects until each component is completed.

When planning a novel, I'd write a short summary of each chapter. With many chapter outlines in front of me, I'd then take the focus off the big picture and start with the first word, the first sentence, the first paragraph, and so on. One word at a time, one paragraph at a time, and one chapter at a time. Seasoned writers don't expect perfection on the first draft. At a high level, you circle back, read the work over and over, edit, elicit feedback and adjust course when necessary. The writing process demonstrates how important a focused approach is to goal-setting, if you want to accomplish something meaningful. The results don't come from magically writing a novel; they come from writing a few hundred or maybe a couple of thousand words per day.

This works the same when planning your life. The compounding effect of tiny bursts of focused effort is how you write the story of your life. So, if you feel aimless and unsure about your future, you may need to figure out what you want, with the *"I want... because..."* method as a first step. Then, with a clear vision, break down your goals into smaller components. Focus only on the first step until it is completed, then move on to step two, and so on. Over time, you'll start to see the puzzle coming together, if you're persistent, committed and have a growth mindset.

Climbing Mount Everest isn't accomplished by just climbing Mount Everest. The first step is learning from the experiences of others who have done it. The second step is planning the finances to make it happen. The third step may be looking far into your schedule, to pick a start date. The fourth step is training. Pretty soon, you'll be flying to Lukla Airport and making the 12-15-day journey to base camp. Then, as the climb becomes more demanding, you focus on one step at a time. The work is done little by little, with short bursts of focused attention, followed by a review of what was accomplished, making adjustments, and then a push forward to the next milestone.

Not only does the *SMART* goals process apply to any goal, but there's another aspect that cannot be overlooked, and that is found in the A.B.C. goal methodology, attributed to Frank L. Smoll, Ph.D.[19]

A.B.C. PROCESS OF GOAL-SETTING:

A = Achievable

B = Believable

C = Committed

Whether you're attempting to run a race, learn a trade, earn a degree, write a book or attempt any worthwhile pursuit, you must believe you can do it, it must be achievable and you must be committed. If you adhere to the beliefs of a growth mindset, you know that almost anything is possible with effort and repetition, so you've got this! This is why having a definite purpose behind your effort is so important. When you push yourself to reach a "stretch" goal, you must be extremely committed to your ultimate purpose. When your purpose is at the core of your values, the commitment will be there. Commitment arises from purpose. Your commitment pushes you forward.

When I think about the power of a greater purpose, and the strength to grind through incredible challenges, I think of single parents. Not only is it amazing because of the overwhelming amount of effort and focus required, but their will to overcome challenges is extremely fascinating. What is their purpose? They do it for their kids, to keep a roof over their heads and make a better life for their family. You see, when you have a compelling motivation, you can do incredible things, and that purpose can make you more committed than you thought possible.

This is true for anyone who works all day in a factory, in the fields or on a construction site. They're committed to grueling, seemingly meaningless, sometimes filthy and physically demanding work, not for the sake of the job itself, but at the core of their commitment is a greater purpose outside of work: to provide for their family, to become financially free, to save for a home, to retire early, or maybe make a better life than they had growing up. It's not always the work that's important, although feeling a sense of accomplishment and doing a great job can be an added perk.

Often, a greater purpose has less to do with the daily work itself, and more about the results after the work is done, such as happy customers, personal accomplishment, financially secure home life, mastering the art of building or fixing something, the joy of buying your child their first bike, or taking your kids fishing, etc.

It will help to connect all your goals with your greater purpose, because they feed off each other, and will energize you to move to the next step in your journey. According to Johnathan Haidt, in *The Happiness Hypothesis: Finding Modern Truth in Ancient Wisdom*, he writes: *"The psychologists Ken Sheldon and Tim Kasser have found that people who are mentally healthy and happy have a higher degree of 'vertical coherence' among their goals – that is, higher-level (long-term) goals and lower-level (immediate) goals all fit together well, so that pursuing one's short-term goals advances the pursuit of long-term goals."*

The laws of becoming collectively add meaning to life. Taking responsibility to become the best possible version of yourself, creating a vision for what you want, and setting meaningful goals in the pursuit of a greater purpose, takes focus, goal-setting and action. But, drilling down into how that actually works is where people get stuck.

For example, many people employ visualization tools, such as meditation, vision boards, or manifesting through repetition of thought and emotion. But science is telling us something new. We know that using visualization tools is a great way to get started, and we can generate the desire for a pursuit by creating a vision board that encapsulates our dream. However, thanks to the work of Emily Balcetis and the Balcetis Lab, we know that you actually double your chance of accomplishing a goal when you think about the consequences of *not* accomplishing your goals – this is called "foreshadowing failure." Turns out, foreshadowing failure – what if your goal isn't achieved – is twice as effective in achieving an objective than only visualizing yourself reaching big goals. This is a huge deal but, when you think about it, it makes sense. And it plays out in the previous example of someone who changes their lifestyle to avoid not seeing their grandkids grow up.

Several scientific studies have proven, over and over, that positive visualization is effective in motivating us to get started in a pursuit, *"...but it actually is a pretty lousy and maybe even counterproductive way of maintaining pursuit of that goal,"* according to Balcetis, among other studies. For example, one study showed that, when people look at a picture of themselves at their current age and envision retiring, they didn't save nearly as much money as the folks who looked at a picture of themselves artificially aged sixty-five or seventy years old. Seeing themselves as much older caused them to save far more money for retirement.[20]

Here are a few more examples that demonstrate how failure foreshadowing can play out:

1. A surprisingly low number of heart-attack survivors actually

change their lifestyle but, those who do change, and focus on meaning and purpose, will tend to live the longest after the event. In a study reported by the *Journal of the American Heart Association*,[21] one survivor stated: *"I have a bucket list for the rest of my life. I focused on things that I really thought I might try and accomplish."* Another survivor said: *"It's that whole thing, you face your mortality, and consider your purpose."* The study showed that many of the survivors did not have a sense of purpose or meaning prior to the attack, but those who took their mortality to heart, and focused on a definite purpose, were among those who lived long after their cardiac arrest. Thinking about what is not accomplished, or left undone in their life, gave them strength and purpose.

2. If you're on a hike in the forest and a large grizzly bear, walking with her cubs, passes you, you will not survive because you think about how great it will be when you're back at the trailhead; no, you will only survive if you think about how horrific it will be when you are being mauled by the bear. Thinking about that will engage all of the neural and physiological changes needed to accomplish the goal of survival.

3. If you don't pass your final exam, you will not graduate. If you don't graduate, you will have to live with your parents and go back to work at The Tasty Freeze.

The idea of foreshadowing failure seems counterintuitive at first, because we've been told how important it is to manifest what we want and focus on the positive output. We've been taught to envision how we'll feel when we hit that goal or accomplish that milestone. But, what if you have a passion or a personal mission that you want to accomplish, and you never do it? What if you never start? How upsetting will that be to you five, ten or twenty years from now? How many lives could have been changed? Would the world have been a better place? Or will the world be worse off if you never go for it? How does that make you feel? Sometimes, foreshadowing failure is far more motivating, because the consequences are too great for us to bear that potential failure.

So, how does foreshadowing failure actually work? Well, it turns out that envisioning ourselves accomplishing a goal makes our physiology respond, by lowering our systolic blood pressure, which puts us in a relaxed state. And we tend to be less active in our pursuit of a goal when we are at ease. But, when we foreshadow failure, and focus on the negative results if we fail, our systolic blood pressure increases, and our amygdala engages a neural pathway that drives us to resolve the stress and anxiety. As a result, we're actually more motivated to take action toward accomplishing a goal, because our physiology encourages movement.

There's a debate about which process is better, and it's a battle between the *"avoidance"* methodology (accomplishing a goal by avoiding negative results) versus the *"approach"* methodology (trying to accomplish a goal by focusing on the positive aspects). I found a great article that tackles this debate by Steve Scott,[22] but ultimately you have to decide if your goals are better achieved by avoidance or approach. Both seem to work based on different types of goals.

In my experience, balancing visualization, manifestation and foreshadowing failure (with action) are unique to your goals and objectives, and your specific motivational needs. There's power in all three methods, so experiment and figure out what works for you.

Balcetis suggests using visualization as a prompt, to get started toward attaining your dream, but use failure foreshadowing as a tool to stay motivated if you want sustained and effective results. Get healthy or die early and your family will suffer. Save money or grow poor and become a burden on your kids. Change or you'll have a sucky life. See how that works? Andrew Huberman has devoted an episode of his podcast to this subject, and interviewed Emily Balcetis in a later episode. You can find his podcasts at *hubermanlab.com*.

Writing specific goals, visualizing, committing, using failure foreshadowing and breaking each objective into manageable steps is the starting point, but there is another key component to accomplishing your goals, which was discovered in the Balcetis Lab: focus.

Focus.

Do you remember the story I told, about me running in the semi-state? I was seconds away from getting into the top ten and failed to reach my goal of going to the state finals. Did I focus? Yes, to a degree. I focused on the runners in front of me, who I wanted to pass, but my focus was on the wrong runners. I needed to focus on beating the tenth-place runner, and I didn't think that way back then. That may have been one of many small mistakes that kept me from reaching that goal.

In Emily Balcetis's lab, they discovered that the key difference between those who reach their goals and those who don't can be traced to the same mistake I made: failure to focus on a single point. She discovered a common trait among world-class runners: the world-class runners had mastered the art of focusing on a single point in front of them, and charging after that target. In other studies, she found that vision plays a big role in how we see our goals, too. In several studies, she found that groups who were instructed to focus on a single point in an exercise would perform much better than those who were told to be aware of their surroundings. They improved performance by 23% and felt 17% less pain.

Once the participants learned the art of focusing their attention, they were equipped to improve their performance outside of the lab, too. This taught Balcetis that anyone who learns the art of focusing, or narrowing their vision on a single point, will have greater success in accomplishing those smaller goals (manageable steps) that add up to the big goals. You can learn more about this study in an interview with Balcetis at *The Knowledge Project*.[23]

Practically speaking, in my sales role, I definitely experienced a decline in performance when there were too many objectives: reports to file, quotes to update, cadences to follow, meetings to attend, product updates, shipments to babysit, finding unavailable equipment, etc. These distracting tasks take away from the ultimate goal: selling. I'd find myself growing my territory and signing up new customers only when I deprioritized the too-many-to-count tasks and distractions. Sometimes you have to remove yourself from distractions, if the tasks are deemed less of a priority. That doesn't mean that you avoid your responsibilities, but you may have to shuffle your schedule, so that you're doing your most important tasks when you are the most energized and motivated. For me, that's in the morning.

Focusing is the only way I can write a book while working a highly demanding profession. Focus takes discipline. It takes intentional time management, by planning my writing times immediately after a morning routine that energizes and invigorates my mental state. My best writing happens early in the morning, so it's critical that I create habits which automate and capitalize on that part of the day, because the goal to finish this book, and others to come, is that important to me.

This is true for you, too, although your goals may require a schedule catered to your unique needs. After analyzing what you want, and breaking the goals into manageable steps, think about when and where you will be the most focused when working on those tasks. The garage? Your home office? In the basement? The library? Time and place matter. If you want to progress through your goals, set yourself up for success by figuring out when and where you can remain the most focused.

It's important to focus on the big picture, and focus on the individual components until each task is complete. If you have trouble focusing on any task for a long period of time, don't look down on yourself; most people can only hold their attention for up to three minutes. You may need to look away for a second. Take a breather. Let your mind drift for a few seconds, and then get back at it. Many people, including myself, have learned to focus in spite of our tendency to be easily distracted. But, when you have an important vision and a strong reason to accomplish it, you remember why you're working on it, and continue toward the objective.

Focus on a single point, figuratively speaking. Focus on the tenth runner. Focus on the goal. Focus on how great it will feel when you accomplish it, and on occasion ruminate on how bad you will feel if you don't accomplish your goals. Add a visual picture, for a constant reminder of your vision. Keeping your goals in front of you, visually on paper

and strategically placed, is so important to staying focused. Out of sight, out of mind is an old cliché, but it's true.

Ultimately, it doesn't matter what mechanism you use for goal-setting; the point is to get your goals out of your head and onto paper, and get laser-focused. That's step one. Step two is breaking goals into manageable steps. The more specific you can be – such as stating exactly what will be accomplished and exactly when you will complete the task – the more likely you are to achieve your goals. And, finally, make your goals meaningful by connecting them to your greater purpose. Foreshadow failure and get your state-of-mind ready to take action, then get laser-focused on the small steps needed to accomplish the bigger picture.

If you look for meaning in the things you want to accomplish, you are more likely to achieve them, and more likely to be happier on the winding road that gets you there, in spite of the obstacles. Becoming your greater purpose requires you to become a better person, more capable and better equipped to succeed. Learning the art of goal-setting, and focusing on the daily disciplines to hit those milestones, will help build confidence in who you are becoming. And you become your greater purpose when you become a better you.

Chapter 11

DEVELOPMENT

"Learn to work harder on yourself than on your job."

Jim Rohn

Once you've taken one hundred percent responsibility for your life, choices and results, defined your vision and the purpose of your vision, and have laid out your goals to accomplish your dream, it's time to begin working on you. Now that you've worked so hard to define what you want, and how you're going to get there, you will discover that the person you are right now may not be capable of achieving some of the steps you outlined in your goals. You may need to learn new skills. You may need to tame some of your personal quirks. You may need to learn new habits, or get rid of old habits that are restricting your growth. You may need to spend some time (days, months or even years) developing yourself as a leader, journeyman, coach, better listener, better communicator, etc. You may need to work on your character by training yourself to be more calm, cool, and collected. You may need to heal your body, get in shape, or clean up your diet so you have the energy to accomplish your greater purpose.

By taking one hundred percent responsibility for becoming your greater purpose, this shouldn't come as a surprise. If the old you and old neural pathways controlled where you were going, then you will need to build a new you, with new neural pathways, to get to the destination you actually want. This will require you to not only "work at personal development", but create a culture of personal development within yourself. A culture of personal development means that you are committed to growing, stretching and developing from this time forward, indefinitely. You don't expect others to develop you. You don't expect others to change. You take one hundred percent responsibility to become the person required to reach your full potential.

Law #5: PERSONAL DEVELOPMENT
Build the person capable of accomplishing your goals.

Whenever you hit a wall, find the tools to climb it. If you don't have a skill needed to reach a milestone, find a resource to learn it. If you don't know where to start, ask someone who's been there. When you're given an answer, take the advice, practice and fail. Start over. Get better. Make a habit of continuously improving.

Unfortunately, we live in a world filled with victims. And thinking of yourself as a victim is the enemy of personal development. You can't master your next skill until you believe that learning that skill is your responsibility, and the sweat and effort required to learn it will make you better and help you get what you want. This process will never end. Just when you think you've learned the right skill, technology changes how it's done. A growth mindset requires that you are flexible, and willing to adapt to new information and new ways of doing things. When you hit a goal, or achieve something on your bucket list, you will discover another weakness, another knowledge gap. In fact, the more you know, the more you know that you *don't* know what you *need* to know. A culture of personal development will help you become better at whatever is needed for you to reach your full potential and become your greater purpose.

Too many people settle for average, and when you're average you cannot reach your full potential or become your greater purpose.

People stay average because they give an average effort. And yet, most people want more for their life. They want better results but refuse to give a better effort. They want more money but refuse to get better skills. They want more training, but leave the responsibility to someone else to start the process. Take a look around; this is why so many people are frustrated, or complain, or play the role of a victim. We blame society. We blame the government. We blame the one percenters, or our partner, or our boss, for our problems.

Can you see why becoming your greater purpose requires all of these steps: taking one hundred percent responsibility; deciding what you want; choosing the purpose; getting laser-focused on your goals? They are required because you cannot get anything you want – besides living your life snuggled up in a fetal position – unless you put forth significant effort. Oh, sure, society will provide a basic education for anyone, and maybe basic housing and basic income, for those who need a little help for a little while, but most people want more than the basics. I don't think you want to settle for barely getting by. I don't think you want to live a life without any sense of meaning or significance, or experiences and relationships that bring happiness.

Mastering the laws of becoming can help anyone get what they want, even if it's just a little more than they have, and if it's for a greater purpose. Therefore, another arrow in your quiver of purpose is personal development. Developing your personality. Developing your talents. Developing your communication skills. Developing your leadership abilities. Developing your listening skills. Developing your role in your relationships. Becoming a better parent, friend, employee, leader or business owner. Whatever role(s) you play will require development if you want more than the basics and something better than you have now.

In John Maxwell's book, *The 21 Irrefutable Laws of Leadership*,[24] law #1 is "The Law of the Lid". This law states that: *"Leadership is the lid to your potential. The lower your leadership ability, the lower the lid on your potential. The higher your leadership ability, the higher the lid on your potential."* And this applies to you whether you're a leader or a follower. The level of your success in any endeavor will be limited by how much effort you put into your personal development. When you grow, your chance of success increases in anything you pursue, whether it's leadership, happiness, purpose, contentment, career or relationships.

For example, if you're struggling in your relationships, you could constantly point fingers at others, but that doesn't usually help anyone. If you find a relationship problematic, developing your communication and listening skills will help you get better results, even if others don't change. When my wife outright told me that my kids have disengaged with me because I wasn't listening to them, my heart shattered into a thousand pieces. That was the first time I put any effort into learning how to become a better listener. Do I still struggle? Yes, I'm easily distracted, but I am developing. I'm becoming. I'm open to change. And there other personal relationship challenges I continue to deal with. However, I'm open to hearing that I have weaknesses and that I need to improve, as painful as it is to hear that I'm failing.

Becoming is developing. Please don't confuse becoming with arriving. You may hit milestones in your life, or be very successful in your field, but you will never stop becoming, improving and developing when you're living your greater purpose.

Too often, people think that they "aren't perfect", so they excuse their failures. They think: *I'm not perfect, so it's okay if I don't try.* They see people who've "made it" and think: *I'm not as perfect as they are, so that's not possible for me.* What many people fail to realize is that no one is perfect. We all have the same problems: health problems, financial problems and problems with our personal relationships. But, where many people go wrong is determining their potential by comparing themselves to others. However, the only difference between highly successful people and the average person is how they deal with their problems. People willing to develop themselves, grow and learn during the trials and tribulations of life, are the ones who progress faster. That's it. For the most part, they're not smarter. They're not privileged. Most millionaires, for example, come from modest, middle-class homes or even impoverished families, but the key difference in their becoming is that they chose personal development as a path to accomplishing something better than where they came from.

We all have weaknesses. Sometimes it's how we relate to others. Sometimes it's something else. Everyone has unique strengths and deficiencies. But, the idea that personal development is only for your financial and professional development is wrong. Personal development is all-encompassing. Becoming your greater purpose requires a better you, in all areas of your life: your health, your relationships, how you use your time, your professional skills, your character, your habits. But don't be overwhelmed by that list. You can't change everything overnight and you don't have to. You're becoming; that takes a lifetime. Start slow. Take baby steps. But start by correcting your habits. Your habits may be the things that have the most power over your progress and personal growth. So, let's address your habits, because if you correct even a few of the habits that are stealing your time, you can see immediate and impactful results.

Habits.

Cell phones are the most powerful weapon on Earth. They have the power to destroy societies, and individual lives, in a short period of time. Porn addiction, for example, because of easy access through a cell phone, can quickly destroy a family. Technological warfare, political influencing by way of social networking and media bias, all impact our emotions and energy. And, yet, these instruments of war can empower the human race, too, because they are simultaneously supercomputers that we can carry in our pockets. They have essentially made us human cyborgs, with access to learn anything at any time, to make us more productive, aware, better educated and connected – all for a low monthly fee! And, yet, we choose to spend hours turning our brains into mush, watching Instagram and TikTok videos. Tick-tock. Tick-tock. Wasting time. Wanting more for our lives, while we sit there for hours, endlessly scrolling. Tick-tock. TikTok. Is it just me, or does it seem like TikTok was aptly named after its intention? To waste our time.

Incidentally, TikTok is very controlled inside China. The original version, only available in China, is called Douyin. It's vastly different from the TikTok version used by the rest of the world. In a February 25, 2023 article in *The New York Post*, by Rikki Schlott,[25] Schlott states: *"The apps are nearly identical – but with one critical difference: users under 14 are required to use Douyin in healthy moderation, on 'teenage mode'. Young, impressionable users are limited to 40 minutes a day between 6 a.m. and 10 p.m., to ensure they get adequate sleep. Endless, zombie-like scrolling is interrupted by mandatory 5-second delays. They're also only shown specially-selected, 'inspiring' content. 'The algorithm is vastly different, promoting science, educational and historical content in China, while making our citizens watch stupid dance videos with the main goal of making us imbeciles,' Nicolas Chaillan, former Air Force and Space Force Chief Software Officer told the Post."*

With so much power and potential, this weapon of mass destruction that we hold in our hands is destroying our dreams. It is killing our potential. Your phone could be the single greatest threat to you becoming your greater purpose, and doing something that impacts humanity and your community.

According to consumer trends reporter Alex Kerai, at *reviews.org*, in a May 9, 2023 article on 2023 cell phone trends [26]:

- *Americans check their phones 144 times per day.*
- *89% of Americans say they check their phones within the first ten minutes of waking up.*
- *75% use their phone on the toilet.*
- *57% consider themselves "addicted" to their phones.*
- *46% use or look at their phone while on a date.*
- *27% use or look at their phone while driving.*
- *Americans spend 4 hours, 25 minutes each day on their cell phones.*

It seems that there's nothing more important than being on our mobile devices. And, yet, we know that people want more from life. We know that people want more meaning and purpose than just scrolling for hours a day. We want what amounts to Maslow's Hierarchy of Needs. In her article, "10 Things We All Want in Life",[27] Anne Marshall states that the top ten things we all want are:

1. *Happiness.*
2. *Health.*
3. *Wealth.*
4. *Security.*
5. *Relationships and harmony.*
6. *Meaningful work.*
7. *To leave a legacy.*
8. *Hope.*
9. *Peace of mind.*
10. *Fulfillment.*

This list of wants sounds like a greater purpose, if you ask me. But, if this is what we want, why do we spend 4 hours and 25 minutes a day screwing around on our phones? When I ask how much time my mindset training students spend scrolling on their devices, it's not unusual that most of them spend two or more hours a day watching mindless and entertaining videos. And yet they agree that they want more from life. They have goals. They want more money and experiences. They want to advance in their careers, and have meaningful relationships and purpose.

The problem is addiction – and we're so easily addicted to the dopamine rush that comes after every thirty-second video. So, if you want a better life, you must learn to master your phone and use it as a tool to get what you want, putting strict controls on your casual use by limiting your screen time.

If your cell is not a problem, that's great. You are an anomaly. Literally everyone I know believes that they spend too much time scrolling through Instagram, Facebook and TikTok, in spite of how much time it's wasting. However, there are plenty of other habits that are killing our dreams. According to The Berkeley Well-Being Institute: *"A habit is any action we perform so often that it becomes almost an involuntary response. If this habit becomes undesirable, we may consider it to be a 'bad habit'."* Some of the examples they cite are smoking, not exercising, not getting enough sleep, too much screen time, negative self-talk and drinking too much alcohol.[28] Any of these habits can be detrimental to reaching your goals and getting what you want. And, if you combine any of these with a couple of hours scrolling, it will be even more difficult to get what you want and become your greater purpose.

We all have the capacity to fall prey to these addictions, to some degree. But the first step to breaking away from your addiction/obsessions is to realize there's a problem. Becoming self-aware that you may have habits which are actively preventing you from getting what you want can be eye-opening.

Try doing the following exercise, to get an understanding of how your habits are keeping you from getting what you want out of life. You can do this exercise by writing what you want on the left, then drawing a line (real or imagined) from the *"What you want"* line to the respective *"Habits preventing progress"* line. If something you want is being prevented by one of your bad habits, you now know what habit(s) you can start working toward removing and/or replacing with habits that will support what you want.

WHAT YOU WANT: **HABITS PREVENTING PROGRESS:**

_____   Scrolling (TikTok or social media)

_____   Sleeping in

_____   Lack of exercise

_____   Excessive drinking/drugs

_____   Netflix binging

_____   Poor diet

_____   Excessive gaming/screen time

_____   Porn

_____   Other:

I love what Brian Tracey said about habits: "Good habits are hard to develop but easy to live with. Bad habits are easy to develop but hard to live with. The habits you have and the habits that have you will determine almost everything you achieve or fail to achieve." Your habits are dictating your future. They are either helping you build the person needed to accomplish your goals or, if they're bad habits, they are preventing you from becoming the person capable of doing incredible things. That's a hard truth to swallow. But, if you're honest with yourself, you know what's true about your habits. Often, bad habits can be something we keep locked behind closed doors, and that makes it really hard to be honest with others and ourselves.

So, how can you change? How do you get rid of bad habits and create helpful habits? In the Berkeley Well-Being article cited above, we learn that: *"...scientists have shown that a 'habit loop' involves a cue, response, and reward which is present in everyone. However, research suggests that you're more likely to fall into this habit loop when you experience negative emotions. These emotions often then become the cues to this habit response. For example, many people report that they'll eat more when they are bored or when they are tired. Other people drink or smoke more when they are stressed out. These negative emotions thus act as the cue that connects to the response and reward of our bad habit."*[29]

MECHANICS OF A HABIT:
Cue + Craving + Response = Reward

To create new habits, that help you get what you want and break out of a bad habit loop, James Clear, author of *Atomic Habits*, suggests the following steps, which can be found on his *Atomic Habits* Summary page [30]:

HOW TO CREATE A GOOD HABIT:
The 1st law (Cue): *Make it obvious.*
The 2nd law (Craving): *Make it attractive.*
The 3rd law (Response): *Make it easy.*
The 4th law (Reward): *Make it satisfying.*

HOW TO BREAK A BAD HABIT:

Inversion of the 1st law (Cue): *Make it invisible.*

Inversion of the 2nd law (Craving): *Make it unattractive.*

Inversion of the 3rd law (Response): *Make it difficult.*

Inversion of the 4th law (Reward): *Make it unsatisfying.*

Clear has helped millions of people improve their lives, and I am one of them. In his book, *Atomic Habits*, he writes: *"Every action you take is a vote for the type of person you wish to become. No single instance will transform your beliefs, but as the votes build up, so does the evidence of your new identity. This is one reason why meaningful change does not require radical change. Small habits can make a meaningful difference by providing evidence of a new identity. And if a change is meaningful, it is actually big. That's the paradox of making small improvements."*[31]

The person you are today didn't arrive overnight. It's taken a lifetime to build the person you've become, whether you're satisfied with that person or not, and it will take time to build the person capable of becoming your greater purpose, if that's what you truly desire. Adjusting your habits may seem like an afterthought when you think about doing great things, but any habit is essentially a neural habit, and those are the things that control your time, thoughts, beliefs, choices and, ultimately, your results. So, don't be deceived. If you've given control of your time, attention and passion to a habit, and the hours spent doing that habit are not helping you get what you want, it's time to let it go. It's time to decide if you're going to win, or if the habit is going to win over you. Is that habit more important than your vision? Is scrolling on your phone for hours more important than accomplishing your goals?

Clear goes on to say: *"The purpose of setting goals is to win the game. The purpose of building systems is to continue playing the game. True long-term thinking is goalless thinking. It's not about any single accomplishment. It is about the cycle of endless refinement and continuous improvement. Ultimately, it is your commitment to the process that will determine your progress."*[32]

If you want to become your greater purpose, you'll have to develop customized habits (a system) to help you build your unique purpose. If your current habits are preventing you from getting what you want from life, read Clear's book, then start the process of creating habits which help build your process (with thoughtful habits) to get you where you want to go. Evaluating your habits is a critical first step in accomplishing anything; many people never get started because the habits they've developed are the things that keep them from taking any action, taking full responsibility or finding the motivation to even think about changing anything.

Take your life back. Take control of your habits. Build new habits that develop you into the person capable of accomplishing your vision. It's your vision. It's your dream. Don't let time-sucking habits keep you from achieving your greater purpose. You have big plans and you'll need the energy, vitality and a clear mind to get that done, so re-engineer your habits into a machine that will give you the capacity to produce big results.

Lifestyle.

You cannot become your greater purpose without addressing your health. To accomplish your most important objectives, you'll need energy, a clear mind, good mental health, longevity and the ability to focus. Taking your health seriously is important to reaching your long-term goals and passing on a legacy to your family. So, if you haven't already addressed the food you're putting into your body, and your lifestyle, it's time to start seriously considering making changes. In order to sustain getting what you want, you will need to create habits that make exercise and eating well part of your daily routine. Here are a few tips to begin taking immediate action:

1. Drink water. Reduce or eliminate pop and energy drink consumption.
2. Exercise/walk 15-30 minutes a day.
3. Reduce or eliminate alcohol and sugar consumption.
4. Spend more time outdoors and get more sunlight.
5. Get better sleep.
6. Reduce or eliminate scrolling on your phone/device.
7. Eat anti-inflammatory foods.
8. Stretching, breathing, meditation, prayer, yoga.
9. Learn what's best for your health; we're all different.

Finding a way to incorporate these simple changes into your daily routine can be easier than you think, and your phone can help you do it. Consider setting alarms to help you start making new habits. I've created some examples, to show you how you can punch in new habits that can develop a healthier you. Do the activity as soon as the alarm goes off. This is only effective if you can set the alarm at a time critical to changing the habit. Do not snooze. Take immediate action within five seconds, as per Mel Robbins's *The 5 Second Rule*.[33]

1. Prep for the next morning before you go to bed.
2. Morning development routine.
3. Drink water.
4. Exercise/walk/stretch.
5. Take deep, relaxing breaths (a feature of Apple Watch).
6. Listen to something positive/motivating/an audiobook (while

walking/driving).

7. Eat healthy.

8. Text someone you love.

9. Listen to an audiobook/podcast while driving home.

10. Reminder to reduce or eliminate alcohol or other vice.

11. Spend time with family/on relationships.

12. Go outside. Get sunshine.

13. Activities to accomplish goal.

14. Eliminate blue light one hour prior to sleep.

15. Chill: well done. Do an activity of your choice.

16. Go to bed. No scrolling. Sleep well.

These are just a few ideas to help supercharge your health habits. I use several of those alarms on my phone to keep me focused, remind me of my priorities, and stick to the habits that are important to accomplishing my goals. They can be a great tool to shock you into changing. Are sixteen alarms overkill? I don't know; you tell me. If there are things you need in your life, to help you get what you want, and you're not doing them, maybe it's time to try something new. Punching in automated reminders, in addition to my morning alarm, works for me. Is there anything in that list that you could bear to improve? Are there meaningful habits that you need to add to the list? Customize your alarms. It's your life! Figure out what you want, and use the notes from previous chapters to determine what you need to prioritize, with regular reminders.

Exercise.

We can't gloss over exercise. Walking and mild exercise could become your superpower. If you add nothing more than a morning walk to your routine, you could begin experiencing life-changing results. I've learned that simply adding 20-30 minutes of walking, jogging and/or some pushups or burpees can help to get my brain and body in an energized state. Walking is my secret weapon. I wake up at around five a.m. and get through a walking/jogging mindset routine, so that I'm ready to write and research every morning by six a.m. I get so much done, have zero distractions, and my heightened state easily puts me in flow, in a good mood, and energizes me for the day. When I go for days or weeks without exercising, my mood and energy can quickly decrease.

Don't trust me; trust the science. Exercise improves your mood, energy, long-term memory and focus, and reduces your risk of depression and other neurological ailments. High performers are almost always aware of their health, exercise and watch their food intake. According to Wendy A. Suzuki, Ph.D., Professor of Neuroscience at NYU: "...*moving your body has immediate, long-lasting and protective benefits for your brain that can last for the rest of your life.*" She goes on to say that science shows: "...*exercise is the most transformative thing that you can do for your brain today.*" How does it work? Wendy goes on to explain that exercise does three important things that can transform your life:

1. Immediately improves brain chemistry: "*A single workout that you do will immediately increase levels of neurotransmitters like dopamine, serotonin and noradrenaline.*" This improves mood and your ability to focus, for at least two full hours.
2. Exercise improves reaction time.
3. Exercise "...*changes the brain's anatomy, physiology and function.*" With only thirty minutes of exercise a day, you can increase the size of the hippocampus and long-term

memory.

Point number three is critical to becoming your greater purpose because, in your journey to create new neural habits that help you get what you want, you need a healthy hippocampus, where new learning takes place and new neural pathways and memories are formed. Therefore, if you want to start overcoming the bad habits that are keeping you from moving toward your greater purpose, start with exercise. If you want more from life, you'll need to transform the way you think, the way you move and the way you eat. Simple exercises like walking or yoga are the easiest ways to start getting your body and mind in shape.

I love what Andrew Huberman said, in an interview on the *Neuro Lifestyle* YouTube channel. Huberman said: "I always think the best way to outperform everybody in your business, or at least keep up in a very competitive business – and Joe Rogan is a beautiful example of this – is to take excellent care of your health... People who are really good at their craft invest in taking really good care of themselves." Want to become your greater purpose? You only need to prioritize a fraction of your day to your mental and physical health, and you can do it in just thirty minutes. If you can add a cold shower or ice bath to your routine, you'll stabilize your mood and emotions, too. However, it's important to speak to your doctor first. This is not medical advice, so do your own research and get professional direction.

Clearly, exercise is one of the key ingredients in mental health and neurological transformation. And, transforming the way you think is the key to changing your life. Awakening and healing your brain will help you see the world in a new light, lift your spirits, give you energy and improve your mood. If your body and emotional state are not in a great place to begin with, how can you entrust your greater purpose to your lesser state? Perhaps what is needed in your life is not figuring out what you want first, but rather getting your mind and body in a better place, as a greater priority, so you can think clearly about what you want and what's really important to you. A poor diet and lack of exercise impact your mood, thoughts and energy, to such a degree that fixing these two areas of your life could be the thing that revitalizes your relationships and motivation, without any of the other steps. You cannot become your greater purpose if your brain and body stay where they are – if you're not living a healthy lifestyle. As the still, soft voice pulls you toward your greater purpose, your brain and body must go with it. Your body is the vessel where the real you resides, so you must nurture it, if not for the sake of your greater purpose, then for the sake of those who you care about.

Exercise.
Mental health.
Healthy food.
Good habits.

These are the foundations to your transformational experience. These are the foundations to getting your body and brain in a place where you are capable of becoming your greater purpose. Taking one hundred percent responsibility, creating your vision, finding your why and getting laser-focused on your goals will do you no good if you don't work on improving your mind and energy. If you care about your greater purpose, you must care for your brain and body, so that you can fulfill your vision. All of these steps work together, but a healthy diet and exercise can accelerate you toward accomplishing your goals, because you'll have more energy, a clear mind and a better mood to help you clean up the other areas of your life.

Developing yourself is not just a theoretical task; it's physical. Your mind, body and soul are all connected, and they all need to be nourished. So, if you're sick and tired of being sick and tired, please take this chapter very seriously.

A Western diet may be your problem. If you don't think much about what you eat, your body won't think much about you. If you've nourished a growth mindset, but it feels like you don't have the energy to go after your dreams, your diet may be the thing preventing you from living out your greater purpose. Not only can your diet degrade your health, but it can impact your mood, motivation and creativity.

In her TED talk, professor of clinical psychology Julia Rucklidge makes science-backed claims that our diet is deteriorating our brains, causing all kinds of neurological ailments, such as psychosis and schizophrenia, and is a major contributor to Alzheimer's Disease.[34] She points out several studies which show that adding dietary patterns affects mental health. A healthy diet is one that is fresh, and high in fruits and vegetables. Rucklidge states: "The more you eat a prudent, or Mediterranean, or unprocessed type of diet, the lower your risk of depression. And, the more you eat the Western diet or processed food, the higher your risk of depression... Not a single study shows that the Western diet is good for our mental health. What is the Western diet? Well, it's one that is heavily processed, high in refined grains, sugary drinks, takeaways, and low in fresh produce. And a healthy diet is one that is fresh, high in fruits and vegetables, high in fish, nuts and healthy fats, and low in processed foods."

Rucklidge is not alone; American author, clinical researcher and Founding President of the Physicians' Committee for Responsible Medicine, Dr. Neal Barnard, has written extensively on the effects of diet and brain health, including the book: *Power Foods for the Brain: An Effective 3-Step Plan to Protect Your Mind and Strengthen Your Memory.* In his TED talk, he summarizes studies showing that diet can increase the chances of dementia and other cognitive diseases, and shows that genetic disorders *"are not destiny".* He encourages a low-carb, healthy fat and colorful vegetarian diet.[35]

In 2023, scientific studies showing the effects of diet on mental health are rapidly emerging. Should you become a vegetarian, go keto, Mediterranean, Adkins, carnivore, or practice intermittent fasting? Finding the answer to that question is part of the personal development journey. Figuring out what works for you and your body is something you'll have to determine for yourself, because we're all different. There is no shortage of books, documentaries and podcasts covering the many benefits of all those diets, and more.

In the Netflix documentary, *The Secrets of the Blue Zone*, we learn that there are several regions across the globe where people tend to live to a hundred years plus. Their lifestyles are much different from the typical Western lifestyle. Host Dan Buettner is one of the world's preeminent experts on centenarians, and the diet and lifestyles that give them superhuman longevity. The docuseries chronicles the diets, movements, geography, relationships and mindset that nurture centenarians, who live decades after most people pass away. It's an eye-opening documentary, that pokes holes in the Western concept of healthy living. You can learn more from Buettner's book, *The Blue Zones Secrets for Living Longer: Lessons from the Healthiest Places on Earth*.[36]

If you want to become your greater purpose, it's important to start taking small steps to improve your health, because your greater purpose is depending on you to live a long life, so that you can make a lasting impact. And you can do this while working on the other steps. You can have great intentions to accomplish big things, but without a healthy body and mind, you may encounter physical and emotional issues that prevent, or at the very least, make it difficult for you to get what you want.

Personal development is not a phase. Personal development is a holistic way of life, one where you're constantly aware of and open to your need to grow, learn and improve your mind, body and soul. It embodies the growth mindset – a mindset that believes the person you are now is not the person you're stuck with. Personal development embraces change. It embraces fear. It embraces pain when you uncover a weakness, a character flaw or a mistake you've made. It's not a system you use to change others; it's a system to make *you* better.

Personal development is transformative, if you stay humble and hungry for growth. It's not something you can accomplish in a week, or over a weekend. Personal development is a lifelong strategy for always becoming. What you are becoming is up to you. You can choose to stay as you are. You can choose to go backward. You can choose to improve a few areas in your life. You can also choose to develop new skills and talents, or competencies in areas you've always been interested in. But, the point to remember is that growing, becoming and developing will serve you best if you make it part of your personal culture.

If you own a business or lead any organization, lead by prioritizing personal development within yourself first. Talk about what you're learning. Talk about your failures and the books you're reading, or the podcasts you're listening to that stimulate thought and change. Talk about a new skill you've learned, not to make your team members feel inadequate, but to demonstrate that it's okay to have a weakness, and that growth is a pathway to improvement. Start with you. Creating a culture of personal development will not only make you more capable, but it will empower your team to develop themselves, as individuals with unique, diverse capabilities that you need for your business to succeed, because you cannot do everything perfectly well. You can become the personal development champion in your company and relationships, not by mandating, but by demonstrating a growth mindset, and living out an internal locus of control and personal development strategy. You can do this in a way that expresses acceptance of others where they are, while communicating the *yet* mentality with a growth mindset. Use a coaching leadership style, instead of a management leadership style. Encourage your team when they are making an effort, not criticizing when they don't hit every goal *yet*. *Yet* is a powerful word, and it has proven to be effective in turning a fixed mindset team into a top-performing team, when a growth mindset culture is in play.

Allow everyone you lead to develop at their own pace, and in their own skin, and into their greater purpose, even if it takes them on a path away from your world; we all have our trails to blaze. Lead by example. Lead your coworkers, team and family by developing yourself first. Don't tell them; show them. And then bring in a third party for mindset training, to teach them how to get what they want, reach their full potential and become their greater purpose. If this book has inspired you, buy a copy for your team.   Join *The Mindset Mission at themindsetmission.com*, and let's work together to make the world a better place, by inspiring anyone you influence to purposefully dream, responsibly develop, focus and take action.

It will be an exciting day when you find yourself living your greater purpose. Let those you love and serve have the same freedom to become their greater purpose, too. Read. Listen. Learn. Grow. Change. Expand your mind. Get better. Think long-term. Becoming your greater purpose is a lifelong journey, no matter how much time you have left on Earth. Can you imagine a world where each generation adopts a culture of personal development? If we collectively embrace a mindset like that, not only will you experience greater meaning in your life, the next generation – your children and grandchildren – will experience even more personal satisfaction.

Chapter 12
ACTION

"Action is the foundational key to all success."

Pablo Picasso

Congratulations! If you've made it this far, you're well on your way to becoming your greater purpose. You've learned what it takes to create a winning mindset, get what you want and reach your full potential, with the exception of one critical step: taking action.

Law #6: ACTION
Bring your vision to life by taking decisive action.

I remember hearing Tony Robbins's booming voice shout from the television: "You have to take massive action!" Listening to him say that for the first time made such an impression on me, that I will never forget this key to becoming my greater purpose. I think my body is still quaking from the sound of Tony's authoritative tone!

Tony, however, is not the only success story that preaches the importance of taking action. Jim Rohn frequented the subject often, and said: "Here's the time to act: when the idea is hot and the emotion is strong." And he's not wrong. What other time will you take action? When you feel like it? When you're less motivated? After you hit snooze? Like that's going to work this time. Yeah, right!

Brian Tracy writes in his book, *Eat That Frog*: *"When you regularly take continuous action toward your most important goals, you activate the Momentum Principle of success. This principle says that although it may take tremendous amounts of energy to overcome inertia and get started initially, it then takes far less energy to keep going."*

Like I said earlier, when I was referring to my writing process, real progress is made one chapter at a time, one paragraph at a time and one word at a time. You don't have to conquer the world to accomplish your goals, but you do have to conquer yourself, and do something each day to keep the momentum going. No matter how small the first step is, a little movement gets you one step closer. Some days you'll get very little done, and some days you'll achieve far more than you imagined.

Becoming is a verb. Becoming requires action. Action follows thought.

Taking action is the only way you'll get anything done. There are many influential individuals who, over time, have spoken on the subject of taking action, because it is core to accomplishing anything of significance. Interestingly, not everyone thinks this way. For this reason alone, I'm at a loss as to why mindset training isn't taught in every school, from an early age. Taking action is a key component to making any dream a reality. Action is the art of converting your imagination into a tangible treasure. This is why movie directors begin every scene with the magical word: "ACTION!" Actions are the seemingly unnoticeable steps that build a future from a fantasy. Action is what creates something from nothing. And, becoming your greater purpose is really an action born out of love, for yourself and others. It stems from creative energy. Action is simply a desire that walks from your mind and out of your body, if you want something bad enough.

Benjamin Franklin said: "Well done is better than well said." And Thomas Jefferson stated: "Do you want to know who you are? Don't ask. Act! Action will delineate and define you." This is true no matter what actions you take – good, bad or no action at all.

Maybe you feel like you never accomplish anything. Or maybe you feel like you're never motivated, or never have enough energy. If this is true, I'd like to challenge you. Maybe no one has ever told you that taking action – any action – is the key to accomplishment and motivation? And, again, maybe your lifestyle and diet are contributing to your lack of energy? Maybe you have a medical condition and you should seek professional help? But, if none of that is true for you, you have to understand that every step you take toward reaching a goal, no matter how seemingly insignificant, will motivate you to take another step, and then another.

This is not new. Going farther back in history, the Bible tells us, in the book of *Daniel*: *"The people who know their God shall stand firm and take action."* Greek philosopher Aristotle said: "We become just by performing just actions, temperate by performing temperate actions, brave by performing brave actions." And I'll add to that, by saying you will become your greater purpose when you start to take purposeful actions. This is true if you want to write a book; the first step is to pick up a piece of paper and a pencil and hold them in your hand – that's step one. If you want to run a marathon, get off the couch. If you want to read a book, turn the page. If you want to learn a language, download an app. If you want to learn an instrument, go to the music store. The first step is never the act of actually accomplishing the goal; the first step is always something more simple: standing; clicking; reaching; walking; listening. Don't let your big idea overwhelm you; just simply take the first step – it's the most important step you can take.

Circling back to Tony Robbins, I want to focus on what he has to say about taking action, because he is the King of Action. Let's look at ten notable quotes from the King of Action, followed by my commentary...

TONY QUOTE #1:
"The path to success is to take massive determined action."

To get what you want and become your greater purpose, you must decide what you want and then commit to accomplishing it. This is a mental step that must be accompanied by a physical step. This is why I started with deciding what you want, taking one hundred percent responsibility, followed by creating your vision: you don't take action without purpose. You need to have a meaningful reason and personal commitment, or your vision will fail. But I don't want that for you, and neither do you. So, start with the mental, emotional and tactical steps, then take massive action.

TONY QUOTE #2:

"The truth of the matter is that there's nothing you can't accomplish, if:
1) You clearly decide what it is that you're absolutely committed to achieving,
2) You're willing to take massive action,
3) You notice what's working or not, and,
4) You continue to change your approach until you achieve what you want, using whatever life gives you along the way."

After taking several small steps, it helps to review your progress. You don't want to finally get motivated to take action, then waste time making the same mistakes, over and over. Plan to take some steps and then review. Take some more steps and review again. Writers do this almost every day: we write a few hundred or thousands of words, then we review it before moving forward. We repeat this cycle over and over, and read our books dozens of times after we think we're done. Then we let others read our work for additional feedback, before we send it to a proofreader and editor. Create your own feedback loop and ask for feedback from others, too.

TONY QUOTE #3:

"A real decision is measured by the fact that you've taken action. No action: you haven't truly decided."

It's really important that you decide what you want, take one hundred percent responsibility to become the person capable of achieving those goals, find the purpose in your vision and plot your course, step by step. But, if you don't take action nothing will change; you'll be right back where you started. Conversely, by taking the slightest action, your entire life can change by the sheer act of taking that first, tiny step. John Maxwell demonstrated this in a seminar he taught, when he showed his audience a three-ring binder he kept from his first course, which he took on personal development. He emphasized that it wasn't the content that changed his life, but rather the step he took to attend the course that changed his life. Action matters. It will change your life, too.

TONY QUOTE #4:

"By changing nothing, nothing changes."

You've come this far. You've been through so much. You're probably one step away from realizing an unimaginable future. Turn back now, and it will seem as if the dream never existed. That's really sad. Take action. Take one more step. Ed Mylett touts the importance of doing "one more" in his book, *The Power of One More.*[37] He states: *"You are one decision away from a totally different life."* And you are also one decision away from not changing your life, too. Without action today, tomorrow will be the same, and the totally different life you are seeking will remain out of reach. Any step today, no matter how small, is a step in the right direction.

TONY QUOTE #5:

"Action is the most important key to any success."

Action is the most important key to success, because ideas, dreams, plans, visions and goals will never become a tangible reality until action is taken. Success starts in your head, but it's meaningless without taking the first steps to bring it to fruition. Regular action, carried out with a definite purpose, pushes you through the many challenges you'll encounter. Without action, doing nothing will be your first problem.

TONY QUOTE #6:

"Resolutions require only words. Results take action."

This is why eighty percent of people fail at keeping their resolutions. Most people fail to take action on their good intentions. Most people fail to act on their dreams. Most people fail to follow through on great ideas. Nikola Tesla's idea for free, global power never came to fruition. Father Pellegrino Maria Ernetti allegedly created the Chronovisor, a mechanism that could see into the past, and is thought to be secured in the Vatican. And then there was the AT&T picture phone – a device you may have never heard of. Action, consistently taken, is what nets results. Words alone go nowhere.

TONY QUOTE #7:

"There's something that happens when we write something down on a physical piece of paper. You become a creator when you write down your goals."

Great ideas are conceived in your imagination, but the minute you write it on a piece of paper (action step #1), an idea begins to take on a life of its own. When you look at that idea, once caged in your brain, and see it on paper in the form of words, the heart of that idea starts beating: *thump-thump, thump-thump.* When you expand on the idea, create an outline, brainstorm, budget and mold the basic concepts into tangible components, the idea sprouts a nervous system, appendages and internal organs. Now your creation is breathing; while still on paper, your idea has come alive. The more action you take to feed and nourish your idea, the sooner you can reach down and raise it to its feet. Soon it will begin walking, producing and touching the lives it was created to impact. That's how important it is to write your ideas. By keeping them in your head, you're caging a wild animal that was meant to be set free.

TONY QUOTE #8:

"You are now at a crossroads. Forget your past. Who are you now? Who have you decided you really are now? Don't think about who you have been. Who are you now? Who have you decided to become? Make this decision consciously. Make it carefully. Make it powerfully. <u>Then act upon it.</u>"

Becoming your greater purpose is about knowing where you came from and learning from the past, but going forward. It's about becoming someone different; someone better; someone driven by a meaningful purpose. Becoming is looking forward, and if you want to move from the past to the future, you can no longer look back. You must look ahead, with plans and purpose, then take one hundred percent responsibility to take the action needed to accomplish your dream. At the end of the day, the idea of becoming your greater purpose cannot stay in a book, or in your head, or on a page. When you read the last page of this book, you must take action. You must engage your imagination, think, dream and take action for the next step of your journey. It's your life; make it count, and take an active role in making it meaningful.

TONY QUOTE #9:

"Take massive action. So many people wait until they have all the answers."

Dr. Martin Luther King Jr. said: "If you can't fly, then run, if you can't run, then walk, if you can't walk, then crawl, but whatever you do, you have to keep moving forward."

You will never have all the answers. You will never know everything. Your greater purpose is unique, so don't compare your life to anyone else's, and don't settle for anyone else's idea of what your life should look like. Figure out what you need to do (action) to get what you want, and develop into the person you were created to become. Accept suggestions and feedback and criticism, because you can always learn from others. But focus on *your* dream, *your* goals, *your* purpose. Be realistic about where you're starting from and grow at your pace. You don't need to run yet, or finish the race; crawling is sufficient, as long as you start moving and keep going.

TONY QUOTE #10:

"I believe life is constantly testing us for our level of commitment, and life's greatest rewards are reserved for those who demonstrate a never-ending commitment to act until they achieve. This level of resolve can move mountains, but it must be constant and consistent. As simplistic as this may sound, it is still the common denominator separating those who live their dreams from those who live in regret."

Changing the way you think, look, perform, learn and love will require action. Moving from the life you're living now to a life filled with purpose requires you to act, to change, to move, to take decisive and massive action. There's nothing passive about a better life. There's nothing passive about living intentionally. The good news is that you can start slow if you need to, or you can blast out of the starting block. It's your call. Just don't sit still. Take a deep breath and do what Mel Robbins suggests in her book, *The 5 Second Rule*: count backward, starting from five – *"five, four, three, two, one..."* – then get up and take action. Do something – anything – to get started.

Mel put it this way: *"Hesitation is the kiss of death. You might hesitate for just a nanosecond, but that's all it takes. That one small hesitation triggers a mental system (of neural pathways) that is designed to stop you. And it happens in less than – you guessed it – five seconds."*[38]

Don't let another day pass you by without writing something down: a goal; a vision; something you're grateful for or want to accomplish. Even one tiny step will move you in the right direction. In the context of this book, here's a simple, three-step action plan to start to get what you want, reach your full potential and become your greater purpose:

QUICK ACTION STEPS FOR DAILY PROGRESS:

Step 1: Grab a pen and notepad.

Step 2: Do at least one of the five things below:

- Make a list of your goals. List three steps you can take. Take the first step.
- Read a chapter from a book. Write three takeaways from what you read.
- Listen to a podcast related to your passion. Write an action step. Do it.
- Go for a walk. Think about what you want. Write your ideas on paper.

- Listen to Jim Rohn, Brian Tracy, Ed Mylett, Mel Robbins, Tony Robbins, Tom Bilyeu, Less Brown, Andrew Huberman or a modern thought leader, and write an action step. Do it.

Step 3: Make a bucket list, and put a completion date on at least one goal.

You can also fill out the *"Daily Development Plan"* found at the back of this book, to quickly get started. This is an easy way for you to begin thinking about your vision and start taking action. All of the steps needed to begin changing your life are included in that fifteen-minute exercise.

If you're ready to take more action, and begin real change, there's a more robust set of action steps you can take to begin the process of getting what you want, reaching your full potential and becoming your greater purpose.

ACTION STEPS FOR LIFE-LONG GROWTH:

Step 1. Commit to the *30-Day Mindset Challenge* (details at end of book).

Step 2. Create a personal development plan after completing the #30daymindsetchallenge.

Step 3. Take your greater purpose to the next level. With a growth mindset, internal locus of control, and mastery over *The 6 Laws of Becoming*, you'll know what to do.

Thinking + Action + Purpose.

If action is your body, thinking is your spirit. Kindle these two with a definite purpose, and you instantaneously erupt into a cosmic force for good; a soul on fire, to do the work of the creator – a work you were specifically designed to complete now, in this lifetime. This combination doesn't only ignite careers, it ignites dreams, organizations, families, relationships and your goals. And it doesn't work only when you have a big, outlandish goal; it works when you apply these truths to everyday events, like how you approach your job, your family, conflict, your hobby and relationships. If you want to become your greater purpose, start by finding the smaller purpose in everything you do, make plans and take action.

Thinking + Action + Purpose. This simple triage is how your greater purpose arises from within you. Of course, your programming, neural pathways, mindset and willingness to take responsibility, develop a vision and set goals come into play, too, but they can all be boiled down to thinking, action and purpose. By developing yourself to be a thinker and planner, with a greater purpose, taking action will seem natural. When you develop your mindset in this way, you'll love what you're doing, no matter what it is.

When you develop, think and take action, you'll find ways to help others, by adding value to them, and in the process become your greater purpose. If you develop your mindset and immerse yourself into the messages that build you up, you'll believe that, "You is smart. You is kind. You is important," and you'll feel hopeful about your future. If you develop the belief that you, and you alone, are responsible for accomplishing your dreams, you can take the weight off the shoulders of anyone you've given that responsibility to in the past. This may take some of the stress off your relationships, and remove anger you may have felt when you were expecting others to make you happy, or give you a sense of meaning.

Look, this is your life. Everyone wants the same things you want. Let everyone else live their life and you live yours. If you're called to help others (when they ask for it), that's great! Go for it! If you want something better for your life, go get it. Stop telling yourself that you can't. Stop shaking your fist at the system; that's not helping. Stop pointing out problems and go fix them. Stop wishing for a purpose and go become it. Ask what you can do to make it happen, and take action.

Chapter 13

BECOMING YOUR GREATER PURPOSE

"The purpose of life is a life of purpose."

Robert Byrne

Becoming your greater purpose is a lifelong journey, indeed. And, developing the mindset to live it out successfully is a challenge all of its own. Your experiences and training, habits and lifestyle can make the journey more difficult, or colorful, or meaningful, depending on your point of view. But, once you embrace your strengths, weaknesses, and vision for your life, you can begin the process of developing into the person capable of accomplishing your dreams. With a little mindset training, and tweaking of your habits, you can start the process of developing into the person required to accomplish your biggest goals.

Becoming your greater purpose isn't one-dimensional, wishful thinking; it requires a healthy mindset, personal responsibility and personal development, like any other successful endeavor, and that's what many spiritual, metaphysical and philosophical books miss when teaching how to find your purpose. Becoming your greater purpose isn't just a belief system you carry around in your head; it's in your body, mind and spirit. You don't find it; you become it over time.

Becoming your greater purpose does not mean that all of a sudden your life will be easy. It doesn't mean that, just because you start a personal development plan, you will no longer experience pain. Au contraire. Life has a way of poking holes in our plans, laughing as it points at our obvious lack of control of the universe. Oh, we will suffer, no doubt about that. Loved ones will pass away. Friends may desert you. Businesses will close and layoffs commence. Economies and governments will come and go. And a small percentage of humans will continue to do insidious and unthinkable acts. But don't lose hope. Each of us has a role to play in offsetting the darkness. You see, you are either on the side of darkness or you are on the side of light. It's a law. Look at our planet: while one half is in the light, the other is in darkness. Hold your hand up to the light. One side is illuminated, the other hides in its shadow.

What side do you want to be on? Do you want to bask in the sun, knowing you're doing your part to make the world a little better, or hide in the shadows, avoiding your opportunity to fulfill your calling? It's a choice we must all make. The moment you notice the world around you is missing something important, something only you can see, something only you are uniquely qualified to implement, you must act. That's your calling. That's your greater purpose. That's the moment you can choose to take an active role in inspiring change, or let your idea fall into the abyss of problems that will never be solved. That's a moment when you choose darkness over light.

When you realize your neural habits are the things that have created the world you live in, and decide you want something better, everything can change. When you believe the life you actually want is possible, everything can change. When you understand your life is nothing more than the results of your beliefs and habits, the chains holding you back will fall to the floor, because you hold the key to those chains. You are, in fact, your own gatekeeper.

Changing your view of yourself, others and the world around you happens the same way it was created: through repetition. The world you experience today is the world you and your influencers have created, by immersing yourself in the same belief systems, the same habits, the same self-talk, the same actions and the same lifestyle. Through repetition you may have carved a rut in life. And, if it doesn't feel right, you can carve another path if you want to. Your thoughts and beliefs are what are steering your course. Take control of your mindset and your thoughts, and you will gain control of your destiny.

By following "The Six Laws of Becoming", you can successfully navigate any dream, take one hundred percent responsibility, create a vision for your life, find the reason for your desire, get laser-focused on your goals, continuously develop and take decisive action. No one succeeds at anything until they get a handle on these laws. As you become your greater purpose you will master "The Six Laws of Becoming".

Going back to the original question I asked at the end of Chapter One, what do you want? What do you *really want* from life? That's where you must start. That's ground zero. What do you want? Do you want something better? Do you want a life that seeks money? Or meaning? Or relationships? Or all of the above? What does that look like? Once you've answered those questions, you now know what to do.

This book does not have all of the answers, but maybe it'll play a small role in your journey of becoming. If that happens, the effort that went into writing this book will be well worth it – not only for me, but for you as well.

Final thoughts.

I intentionally tried not to over-spiritualize this book, because I respect all of your beliefs, and I intentionally wanted to get into the science of mindset training because it's significant. I will have failed, however, if I overlook the spiritual side of becoming your greater purpose. I'm not pushing religion, but I would be inauthentic if I didn't share the spiritual side of my journey.

I believe we were all created for a specific purpose in history, a purpose specifically formed by an intelligent designer. Some people call it God, some call it Universal Source, the Universe, or a plethora of other titles. The Bible says, in *Psalm 139:13-14:* "*For you formed my inward parts; you knitted me together in my mother's womb. I praise you, for I am fearfully and wonderfully made.*" In *Proverbs 16:4*, it says: "*The LORD has made everything for its purpose.*" The verse in *Jeremiah 29:11* states: "*For I know the plans I have for you,' says the Lord. 'Plans to prosper you and not to harm you, plans to give you hope and a future.'*" And *Proverbs 20:5* declares: "*The purposes of a person's heart are deep waters, but one who has insight draws them out.*"

Clearly, the Bible has a lot to say about why we are here and God's intended purpose for your life. But there are other ways to look at life and purpose, and I fully understand that. We live in a big world, with a variety of ideas, philosophies and unique belief systems. I believe God wired me to do something meaningful, but there are other ways to look at purpose.

In Japan, they have a term to describe the concept of purpose and meaning. They call it "ikigai" (ee-key-guy). Ikigai is embedded in Japanese culture, mindset, and their purpose for physical and emotional well-being. Ken Mogi, the author of *Awakening Your Ikigai*, said ikigai is "a reason to get up in the morning," and "waking up to joy". It's a beautiful way to see the world and your purpose in it.[39]

There is an endless inventory of viewpoints. Russian cultures often find meaning in a blend of Orthodox Christianity, traditional Slavic beliefs and a sense of national identity, emphasizing family, community and contributions to the greater society. Canada's concept of purpose and meaning is diverse, embracing the value of inclusivity, multiculturalism and individual fulfillment, while respecting the country's First Nation's spiritual beliefs and values. Brazilian culture is a fusion of indigenous, African and European influences. There, purpose and meaning are often seen in the celebration of life, community and spirituality, with Afro-Brazilian religions and Catholicism playing significant roles. Australia's indigenous cultures, such as Aboriginal and Torres Strait Islander peoples, value a deep connection to land and ancestors, finding purpose and meaning through preserving cultural heritage and spiritual practices. Costa Ricans live by the Pura Veda philosophy of living positively, in spite of life's challenges.

Many Native American cultures, like the Lakota (Teton Sioux), seek their greater purpose in a custom called Hanbleceya: crying for a vision. This is the traditional idea of a "vision quest", where a young person travels into the mountains and asks the Great Spirit to show them the vision for their life. It's a time of quiet reflection and listening to the Spirit's voice. It's a beautiful culture of "becoming."

Seeking a vision has gotten lost in the hustle and bustle of our modern world, but we need it back. You need it back. We all need to seek our vision and become our greater purpose.

We all have different cultures and backgrounds that make us unique. Here in the United States, our family traditions are a melting pot of beliefs from all over the world. We value individual liberty, freedom to discover our possibilities, faith, new ideas and freedom to explore our creativity. We find purpose in our family, spiritual identity, heritage, work and leisure.

If you're young and willing to learn from others, you will fast-forward the becoming process. Now that you have the tools for a winning mindset and understand "The Six Laws of Becoming", you can get laser-focused on becoming whatever you desire, and have plenty of time to change, grow and become someone new, as you progress through life. I hope my story has resonated with you. I hope I have inspired you to carefully consider who you are becoming and what you let into your thoughts, because the habits and choices you make now, if repeated unchecked, can create a person you may not want to become. Feed your mind with what you want and follow "The Six Laws of Becoming". And please let me know if this book has impacted your life.

If you're a parent, this phase in your life may require you to pursue multiple purposes: a purpose for your work, a purpose in your marriage and a purpose for your children. You will need to find a healthy balance among all of these entities. Your work has a purpose to serve the marketplace. Your marriage has a purpose, perhaps, to complement your spouse and build a life together. As a parent, part of your purpose is to love and help your children discover their talents and strengths. Balancing life isn't easy. It requires a team. It requires intention. It requires you to pursue your vision while simultaneously and meaningfully serving in other capacities. And, if your vision requires you to pursue a side hustle, you'll need to be extra cautious that you don't let your greater purpose overtake your other obligations, until the time is right to make it your greatest priority.

In closing, anyone can get what they want, reach their full potential and become their greater purpose. It's not easy. It may take you months, or even a lifetime. But, what's important is that you're grateful for the journey, and appreciate every moment of your becoming. It doesn't matter how you were trained in your formable years, or what type of mindset you learned, you can change if you want to. Through effort and repetition, you can learn a new way of thinking, a new way of seeing the world and a new way of seeing yourself.

Discovering what you really want from life is a matter of knowing what's out there. If you grow up in a small town, and haven't experienced other parts of the world or met people from different cultures, how will you know what you want? If you've come from a big city, you have no idea what it's like to live in a small town, with no one around for miles and no jobs available. Without a variety of experiences, you can hardly discover all that there is to know about yourself, potential occupations and the world.

So, how do you know what road to take? How do you know who you truly are? The answer to that question is *experience*. The more you experience, the more you learn. The more you learn, the more you're open to trying new things. When you're open to new experiences, you'll increase your chance of finding something that gets you in flow and lights up your soul. And that process, the entire process of your life, is really just a journey of discovering who it is you were meant to become. And that person is your greater purpose.

After searching for over fifty years, what I finally learned was that my purpose wasn't found in a job, or a title, or in an accomplishment. My greater purpose was found in discovering <u>who I am</u>, and I would have never found that person had I not traveled down so many rocky trails. I wouldn't have found that person if I hadn't experienced a variety of occupations, or made mistakes, or felt pain, shame, joy, love, failure and victory. What I thought were obstacles were actually just a series of trails, which were leading me to the crest of the mountain. And the rocks and caves were simply the parts of me that needed polishing and refining. You see, it's in living that we discover what life is all about. And it's in trying and failing that we learn what we're really made of.

Now that I'm a dad and a husband, I have an incredible respect for my parents and all they did for me. Although life was hard, and they had their own shadows to deal with, they did the best they could, and they have repeatedly told me how proud they are of me and that they love me. I can honestly say that I dearly love and respect them both. By forgiving them and finding the good in them, I'm free to grow into the person I was created to become. I could choose to be bitter about the past, but I have chosen to be "better", and to appreciate them for the good things they instilled in me.

If you're struggling with finding clarity, or pinpointing exactly what you should be doing with your life, take a breather. Relax. Spend some time alone and think about who you are, and what kind of mindset you have. If you're open to learning and trying new things, just keep moving forward. The more you experience, the closer you get to becoming your greater purpose. Try new things. Take risks. Travel when you can. And fearlessly explore the world.

If you have a fixed mindset, I suggest you work on that. Learn to apply Carol Dweck's five beliefs of a growth mindset, develop an internal locus of control and take one hundred percent responsibility for your life, choices and results. Failure is good. Learning and trying is what builds a better you, not avoiding failure. It's important that you take the pen of your life back from anyone you've given it to, and start writing your own story. No one owes you anything. Don't be a victim. You're the author of your life. You have to believe that, if you want to become your greater purpose.

You can go anywhere. You can do anything. You can be whatever you want to become, if you have the right mindset and apply "The Six Laws of Becoming". If you truly believe that, then I've accomplished what I set out to do in this book: teach mindset training, to help you get what you want and reach your full potential. But, the journey doesn't end here; it will continue for you and it will continue for me, too. We are all learning, we are all developing and we are all becoming. What you become is up to you.

I hope our journey together was fulfilling and helpful. I hope your life is better as a result of reading this book. My greatest desire is for you to get what you want, reach your full potential and become your greater purpose. By writing this book, I am becoming my greater purpose. God willing, I hope you become yours, too.

Thank you so much for reading; I appreciate you so much. If you found this book helpful, please share it with your family, teens, college students, employer, friends and coworkers; you never know who needs to hear this message. By sharing what you've learned and encouraging others to read this book, you just might play a small role in transforming a life. And, please write a review, so the algorithms will push it into the hands of anyone else who may be searching for their greater purpose. Thank you!

NOW WHAT?

Now that you've finished the book, you're ready to change and you're eager to establish a vision for your life and start building it. What do you do now? Here are a few suggestions:

1. Go to Amazon and buy a print copy of *The 30-Day Mindset Challenge.* Or go to *themindsetmission.com* to get a free copy of *The 30-Day Mindset Challenge.* This free .pdf will help get you started on building a winning mindset, and on a path to life-changing personal development.

2. If you haven't done so, work through all of the exercises in this book. If you have a digital or audio version of this book, working through *The 30-Day Mindset Challenge* will suffice.

3. Start reading from my suggested reading list found on the next page.

4. Write a review for this book and share it with your friends, family and coworkers.

5. Coordinate a mindset training workshop with your employer or local community leaders, by contacting *themindsetmission.com.* We can help you get started.

6. Make a copy of the *"Daily Development Plan", available FREE at themindsetmission.com,* or create your own customized daily development plan.

SUGGESTED READING LIST

1. *Mindset: The New Psychology of Success*, by Carol S. Dweck.
2. *The Power of One More*, by Ed Mylett.
3. *The High 5 Habit* and *The 5 Second Rule*, both by Mel Robbins.
4. *How to Develop Your Personal Mission Statement*, by Stephen R. Covey.
5. *Can't Hurt Me*, by David Goggins.
6. *The Miracle Morning*, by Hal Elrod.
7. *Secrets of the Millionaire Mind*, by T. Harv Eker.
8. *Everyday Millionaires*, by Chris Hogan.
9. *Think and Grow Rich*, by Napoleon Hill.
10. *Atomic Habits*, by James Clear.
11. *The 21 Irrefutable Laws of Leadership*, by John C. Maxwell.
12. *Change Your Thinking, Change Your Life*, by Brian Tracy.
13. *21 Success Secrets of Self-Made Millionaires*, by Brian Tracy.
14. *Man's Search for Meaning*, by Viktor Frankl.
15. *Cultivating an Unshakeable Character*, by Jim Rohn.
16. *7 Strategies for Wealth and Happiness*, by Jim Rohn.
17. *The Magic of Thinking Big*, by David J. Schwartz.
18. *The Purpose-Driven Life*, by Rick Warren.
19. *Freedom from Fear*, by Mark Matteson.
20. *Start with WHY*, by Simon Sinek.
21. *Psycho-Cybernetics*, by Maxwell Maltz.
22. *Awaken the Giant Within*, by Tony Robbins.
23. *The Blue Zones Secrets for Living Longer*, by Dan Buettner.
24. *Reframe Your Brain: The User Interface for Happiness and Success*, by Scott Adams.
25. *The Holy Bible.*

DAILY DEVELOPMENT PLAN

What I want:

_____

Why I want it:

_____

DAILY RITUAL:

Read _____

for _____ minutes.

Exercise by doing _____

for _____ minutes.

One thing I'm improving this week:

_____

Memorable quote:

_____

What I'm developing in me now:

_____

GOALS:

Daily goal:

_____

Weekly goal:

_____

Monthly goal:

_____

Yesterday's accomplishment:

_____

PERSONAL LONG-TERM GOALS:

Family:
- -
Personal:
- -
Health:
- -
Wealth:
- -

THREE THINGS I'M GRATEFUL FOR TODAY:

1. -
2. -
3. -

HOW I GET WHAT I WANT, REACH MY FULL POTENTIAL AND BECOME MY GREATER PURPOSE:

- Develop a growth mindset and internal locus of control.
- Define my vision – what do I want?
- Take 100% responsibility to accomplish it.
- Get laser-focused on my goals. Organize them in manageable steps.
- Find the greater purpose – my *why* – for direction and strength to overcome.
- Continuously develop and create habits that help me get what I want.
- Take decisive action.

REFERENCES

[1] "Infant Neural Pathways",
https://developingchild.harvard.edu/resources/inbrief-science-of-ecd/

[2] *C.G. Jung Letters, Vol. I*, Page 33.

[3] *On Repetition, Psychoanalysis and Repetition: Why Do We Keep Making the Same Mistakes*, by Juan-David Nasio, page 2.

[4] *On Resilience, The Way Out: A Revolutionary, Scientifically Proven Approach to Healing Chronic Pain*, by Alan Gordon, page 147.

[5] "National Study of Millionaires", Ramsey Solutions.
https://www.ramseysolutions.com/retirement/the-national-study-of-millionaires-research

[6] "Happiness with purpose", Bronk, K. C., Hill, P. L., Lapsley, D. K., Talib, N., & Finch, H. (2009). "Purpose, hope, and life satisfaction in three age groups", *The Journal of Positive Psychology*, 4, 500–510.

[7] "Imposter syndrome",
https://www.medicalnewstoday.com/articles/321730#risk-factors

[8] https://fs.blog/carol-dweck-mindset/

[9] "Mindset perceptions", https://neuroscience.stanford.edu/news/reality-constructed-your-brain-here-s-what-means-and-why-it-matters

[10] "Neural plasticity",
https://www.ncbi.nlm.nih.gov/pmc/articles/PMC6128435/

[11] Ed Mylett on *Confidence*,
https://youtube.com/shorts/gSiBI9OWtyU?feature=share

[12] Dr. Hugo Kehr on *Mind, Heart, and Hand*: https://youtu.be/iuIisjRIcV

[13] *Vision Statement: How to Develop Your Personal Vision Statement*, by Stephen R. Covey, p.10 in e-book version.

[14] Ed Mylett on *Uncovering Purpose*:
https://www.youtube.com/watch?v=ZQvi7kPLVuQ&t=967s

[15] Jackie Swift's article on "The impact of purpose":
https://research.cornell.edu/news-features/benefits-having-sense-purpose

[16] "The science of living with purpose" by Claire Gauen:
https://artsci.wustl.edu/ampersand/science-living-purpose

[17] "The science behind the powerful benefits of having a purpose", by Majid Fotuhi, MD, Ph.D. and Sara Mehr:
https://practicalneurology.com/articles/2015-sept/the-science-behind-the-powerful-benefits-of-having-a-purpose

[18] *Why People Fail to Achieve Their Goals*, by Douglas Vermeenen:
https://www.reliableplant.com/Read/8259/fail-achieve-goals

[19] Frank L. Smoll on "A.B.C.s of goal-setting",
https://positivepsychology.com/goal-setting-
psychology/#:~:text=Smoll%20said%20that%20effective%20goals,C%20–
%20Committed

[20] Dr. Emily Balcetis's study, Balcetis, E., Riccio, M. T., Duncan, D. T., &
Cole, S. (2020): "Keeping the goal in sight: Testing the influence of
narrowed visual attention on physical activity", *Personality and Social
Psychology Bulletin*, 46(3), 485–496.

[21] Study on heart-attack patients: *Qualitative Study of Long-Term Cardiac
Arrest Survivors' Challenges and Recommendations for Improving
Survivorship*, Alex Presciutti, Bonnie Siry-Bove, Mary M. Newman,
Jonathan Elmer, Jim Grigsby, Kevin S. Masters, Jonathan A. Shaffer,
Ana-Maria Vranceanu and Sarah M. Perman. Originally published 8 Jul,
2022
https://www.ahajournals.org/doi/10.1161/JAHA.121.025713#d1e1578

[22] "Approach or avoidance", by Steve Scott:
https://www.happierhuman.com/approach-or-avoidance/

[23] Emily Balcetis on "Goal setting" at *The Knowledge Project*:
https://www.youtube.com/watch?v=bYAe0zXt8xg&t=1292

[24] "The Law of the Lid", *The 21 Irrefutable Laws of Leadership, 25th
Anniversary Edition*, by John C. Maxwell, pg. 1, published by Harper
Collins Leadership 2022.

[25] "China is hurting our kids with TikTok but protecting its own youth with
Douyin", by Rikki Schlott: https://nypost.com/2023/02/25/china-is-
hurting-us-kids-with-tiktok-but-protecting-its-own/

[26] "2023 cell phone usage statistics: Mornings are for notifications" by
Alex Kerai : https://www.reviews.org/mobile/cell-phone-addiction/

[27] "10 things we all want out of life", by Anne Marshall,
https://onehappyplace.org/10-things-we-all-want-in-life/

[28] The Berkeley Well-Being Institute on "Habits" 1,
https://www.berkeleywellbeing.com/bad-habits.html

[29] The Berkeley Well-Being Institute on "Habits" 2,
https://www.berkeleywellbeing.com/bad-habits.html

[30] *Atomic Habits* by James Clear, https://jamesclear.com/atomic-habits-
summary

[31] *Atomic Habits* by James Clear, page 38.

[32] *Atomic Habits* by James Clear, page 27.

[33] *The 5-Second Rule*, by Mel Robbins. https://www.amazon.com/Second-
Rule-Transform-Confidence-Everyday/dp/1682612384

[34] TED talk: "The surprisingly dramatic role of nutrition in mental health", by Julia Rucklidge.
https://youtu.be/3dqXHHCc5lA?si=avqQbRNpE38NO309

[35] TED talk: "Power foods for the brain", by Neal Barnard.
https://youtu.be/v_ONFix_e4k?si=vY7QLrupusLObkQR

[36] *The Blue Zones Secrets for Living Longer (Blue Zones, The); Kindle Edition*, by Dan Buettner. https://www.amazon.com/Blue-Zones-Secrets-Living-Longer-ebook/dp/B0BXBF7N4N/ref=sr_1_4?crid=QXFQGO3D1HHS&keywords=blue+zones&qid=1695474751&s=digital-text&sprefix=blue+zones%2Cdigital-text%2C113&sr=1-4

[37] *The Power of One More: The Ultimate Guide to Happiness and Success*, by Ed Mylett. https://www.amazon.com/Power-One-More-Ultimate-Happiness-ebook/dp/B09VCPHH8W/ref=tmm_kin_swatch_0?_encoding=UTF8&qid=1695478567&sr=1-1

[38] *The 5-Second Rule: Transform Your Life, Work, and Confidence with Everyday Courage*, by Mel Robbins.
https://www.amazon.com/Second-Rule-Transform-Confidence-Everyday/dp/1682612384

[39] *Awakening Your Ikigai: How the Japanese Wake Up to Joy and Purpose Every Day (Kindle Edition)*, by Ken Mogi,
https://www.amazon.com/Awakening-Your-Ikigai-Japanese-Purpose-ebook/dp/B077MX1JF7